Betty Crocker

simply
dessert

100 Recipes for the Way You Really Cook

JG PRESS

contents

The Basics of Cookies and Bars

Who doesn't love homemade cookies and bars? Not only are they easy to bake, they're also portable and fun to eat.

Mixing Cookies and Bars

- Use the stick form of butter or margarine for best results. Tubs of margarine, whipped butter or butter blends contain more water and/or air and less fat, so cookies made with them will be soft, puffy, and tough and will dry out quickly.

- Most cookie and bar recipes call for softened butter or margarine. Perfectly softened butter should give gently to pressure (you should be able to leave a fingerprint and slight indentation on the butter), but it shouldn't be soft in appearance. Butter that is too soft or melted results in dough that is too soft, causing cookies to spread too much during baking. You can let butter soften at room temperature for 30 to 45 minutes, or soften it in the microwave.

- An electric mixer or a wooden spoon can be used to mix dough for most cookie and bar recipes. Sugar, fats and liquid can easily be mixed together with an electric mixer. Flour and other dry ingredients should be mixed on very low speed or by hand to prevent overmixing, which can result in tougher cookies.

Storing Cookies and Bars

To keep those just-baked cookies as fresh as possible:

- Store crisp cookies at room temperature in a loosely covered container.

- Store chewy and soft cookies at room temperature in resealable plastic food-storage bags or tightly covered containers.

- Don't store crisp and chewy or soft cookies together in the same container; the crisp cookies will become soft.

- Let frosted or decorated cookies set or harden before storing; store them between layers of waxed paper, plastic wrap or foil.

- Freeze cookies and bars, tightly wrapped and labeled. Freeze unfrosted cookies up to twelve months and frosted cookies up to three months. Put delicate frosted or decorated cookies in single layers in freezer containers, and cover with waxed paper before adding another layer.

The Basics of Cakes

Any occasion can call for cake, from birthdays to weddings to just surprising the family with a homemade treat. There are almost as many cakes as there are days to celebrate with them.

Mixing Cakes

The recipes in this book call for a hand-held electric mixer. If using a heavy-duty stand mixer, follow the manufacturer's directions on speed settings; overmixing the batter causes tunnels or a sunken center.

You can also mix cake batter by hand with a wooden spoon. Stir the ingredients until they're well combined, then beat 150 strokes for each minute of beating time (3 minutes = 450 strokes). Just be sure to beat the batter for enough time—if a cake isn't beaten long enough, it will be lower in volume.

Baking Cakes

- Shiny metal pans are the best choice for baking cakes. They reflect heat away from the cake for a tender, light brown crust.

- Use the pan size recommended in the recipe. To determine the size of your pan, measure the length and width from *inside* edge to *inside* edge; not across the bottom of the pan. If the pan is too large, the cake will fall flat and may overbake. If it is too small, the cake may bake over the edges and not bake fully in the center.

- Only fill cake pans halfway. To determine how much batter a specialty pan (such as heart-shaped) can hold, fill it with water, then measure the water. Use half that amount of batter. Make cupcakes with any extra batter.

- Bake cakes on an oven rack placed in the center of the oven.

- Cakes are done when a toothpick poked in the center comes out clean. Cool cakes completely on a wire rack away from drafts before frosting or cutting. Serve cakes warm only when the recipe suggests it.

Frosting Cakes

- Cool cakes completely before frosting them. On a hot cake, the frosting will become too soft or melt.

- Frosting should be soft enough to spread without running down the sides of the cake. If frosting is too stiff, it will pull and tear the cake surface, adding crumbs to the frosting. If frosting is too thin, add more powdered sugar, a couple of tablespoons at a time; if too thick, add a few drops of water or milk.

- Stick butter, margarine or butter blends are recommended for frostings. Tubs of margarine, whipped butter or butter blends contain more water and/or air and less fat, so frostings made with them are too soft.

- For easier frosting, use a flexible metal spatula. A light touch helps prevent cake layers from sliding and squishing the filling from between the layers.

Storing Cakes

- Cool unfrosted cakes completely before covering and storing to keep the top from becoming sticky.

- Store cakes with creamy powdered sugar frostings at room temperature, loosely covered with foil, plastic wrap or waxed paper or in a "cake saver."

- During humid weather, refrigerate cakes with very moist ingredients, such as chopped apples, applesauce, shredded carrots or zucchini, banana or pumpkin. If stored at room temperature, mold can grow quickly.

- Store cakes with cream cheese frostings or whipped cream toppings or fillings in the refrigerator.

The Basics of Pies

Everyone loves pie, and baking great pies doesn't have to be hard. Even a beginning baker can make a blue-ribbon pie with just a little practice and these expert tips.

Easy-Does-It Mixing

- Use the type of fat called for in the recipe; shortening is the type of fat most often used and results in a flaky crust. Pastry and crusts contain enough fat that you don't have to grease pie plates.

- With a fork or pastry blender, cut shortening into flour and salt until particles are the size of small peas.

- Mix the dough only until all ingredients are worked in. If you overwork pastry dough, it can become tough.

- For easier rolling, after you've made the pastry dough and shaped it into a flattened round, wrap it tightly and refrigerate for at least 45 minutes or overnight. This helps the fat to solidify (for a flakier crust), the gluten to relax and the moisture to be absorbed evenly.

Rolling Pastry

- With a floured rolling pin, roll the pastry on a lightly floured surface or pastry cloth into a circle that's two inches larger than the upside-down pie plate you are using.

- Roll the pastry from the center to the outside edge in all directions, lifting and turning pastry occasionally to keep it from sticking. To keep the edge from becoming too thin, use less pressure on the rolling pin as it approaches the edge. If the pastry begins to stick, rub more flour, a little at a time, on the rolling surface and rolling pin.

- To transfer pastry to pie plate, fold pastry into fourths; place it in the pie plate with the point in the center of the plate. Unfold and gently ease into the plate. Or you can roll the pastry loosely around the rolling pin and transfer to the pie plate. Unroll pastry and ease into plate. Be careful not to stretch pastry, or it will shrink when baked.

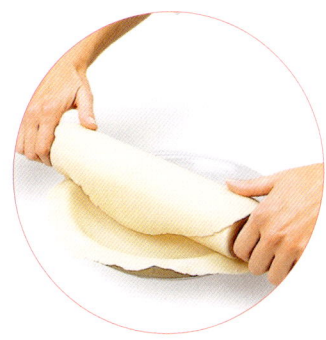

Baking Pies

- Choose a heat-resistant glass pie plate or a dull-finish aluminum pie pan; don't use a shiny pie pan—your pie will have a soggy bottom crust. The most common pie plate size is 9 inches.

- Pies are baked at high temperatures (375°F to 425°F) so the rich pastry becomes flaky and golden brown and the filling cooks all the way through.

- To prevent the edge of the crust from getting too brown, cover it before baking with a strip of foil carefully folded over the edge, or use an edge protector ring. Remove the foil 15 minutes before the end of the bake time so the edge browns.

- If the top crust is getting too brown and the pie isn't done, place a piece of foil on top of the pie to help prevent further browning.

Storing Pies

- Store pies that contain eggs, such as pumpkin and cream pies, in the refrigerator and use within three to five days.

- Fruit pies and pecan pies can be loosely covered and stored at room temperature up to three days.

Freezing Pies

Many pies can be frozen. Pecan and pumpkin pies need to be baked before freezing; fruit pies can be frozen unbaked or baked. Use these tips when freezing pies:

- Cream pies, custard pies and pies with meringue toppings can't be frozen because they break down and become watery.

- Cool baked pies completely before freezing. Place pies in the freezer uncovered. When completely frozen, wrap tightly in foil or place in a resealable plastic freezer bag.

- Freeze baked pies up to four months; unbaked pies up to three months.

Banana–Chocolate Mousse Tart, page 115

- To heat *unbaked* pies: Unwrap and bake frozen pie at 475°F for 15 minutes; reduce oven temperature to 375°F and bake for 45 minutes longer or until center is bubbly.

- To heat *baked* pies: Unwrap and bake frozen pie at 325°F for 45 minutes or until thawed and warm.

Peach-Pecan Cobbler

Peach and Blueberry Crisp with Crunchy Nut Topping

Peachy Pear-Coconut Crumble

Tart Red-Fruit Crisp

Roasted Almond-Cranberry-Pear Crisp

Two-Berry Crisp with Pecan Streusel Topping

Razzle-Dazzle Berry Shortcake

Strawberries with Cheesecake Cream

Baked Apples with Rum-Caramel Sauce

Chocolate Mousse

Easy Tiramisù

Fudge Pudding Cake with Ice Cream

Crème Brûlée

Slow Cooker White Chocolate Bread Pudding

Raspberry Bread Pudding

Chocolate-Strawberry-Walnut Crumble Dessert

Light 'n' Creamy Tropical Dessert

Chocolate Mousse Brownie Dessert

1

dessert in a dish

Peach-Pecan Cobbler

Prep Time: 15 min ■ Start to Finish: 1 hr 35 min ■ 15 Servings

½ cup butter or margarine
3 cans (15 oz each) sliced peaches in light syrup, drained and 1 cup syrup reserved
1 package yellow cake mix with pudding in the mix
1 teaspoon ground cinnamon
⅛ teaspoon ground nutmeg
2 eggs
1 cup chopped pecans
1 tablespoon sugar

1 Heat oven to 375°F. Place butter in 13×9-inch pan and place in oven until butter is melted. Place peach slices on paper towels to absorb liquid.

2 In large bowl, mix cake mix, cinnamon, nutmeg, eggs and 1 cup reserved peach syrup with spoon until well blended. Drop batter by spoonfuls over butter in pan; spread slightly without stirring. Arrange peaches over batter.

3 Bake 30 minutes. Sprinkle with pecans and sugar. Bake 15 to 20 minutes longer or until edges are deep golden brown and center springs back when lightly touched in center. Cool 30 minutes. Serve warm or cool.

1 Serving: Calories 350 (Calories from Fat 140); Total Fat 16g (Saturated Fat 4.5g); Cholesterol 45mg; Sodium 290mg; Total Carbohydrate 50g (Dietary Fiber 2g); Protein 3g

Peachy Pear-Coconut Crumble

Prep Time: 20 min ■ Start to Finish: 1 hr 5 min ■ 10 Servings

1 cup all-purpose flour
¾ cup sugar
¼ cup butter or margarine, softened
1 egg, beaten
1 can (29 oz) sliced peaches in heavy syrup, drained and ½ cup syrup reserved
1 can (29 oz) sliced pears in syrup, drained and ½ cup syrup reserved
3 tablespoons cornstarch
½ teaspoon almond extract
½ cup maraschino cherries, halved and drained
¼ cup flaked coconut

1 Heat oven to 400°F. In medium bowl, mix flour and sugar. With fork or pastry blender, cut in butter, until mixture is crumbly. Stir in egg; set aside.

2 In 1-quart saucepan, mix reserved peach and pear syrups and the cornstarch. Cook over medium heat, stirring constantly, until mixture boils and thickens. Stir in almond extract.

3 In ungreased 12×8 or 11×7-inch glass baking dish, mix peaches, pears and cherries. Stir in syrup mixture. Crumble and spoon flour mixture evenly over fruit mixture.

4 Bake 40 to 45 minutes, sprinkling with coconut for last 10 minutes of baking, until topping is deep golden brown and fruit is bubbly.

A crumble is a British dessert in which fruit is topped with a crumbly pastry mixture and baked.

1 Serving: Calories 360 (Calories from Fat 60); Total Fat 6g (Saturated Fat 3g); Cholesterol 35mg; Sodium 50mg; Total Carbohydrate 74g (Dietary Fiber 3g); Protein 3g

Tart Red-Fruit Crisp

Prep Time: 20 min ■ Start to Finish: 55 min ■ 8 Servings

Fruit Mixture

1 can (14.5 oz) tart red cherries, drained, juice reserved
⅔ cup granulated sugar
¼ cup cornstarch
½ teaspoon ground cinnamon
2 cups fresh or frozen raspberries
1 cup fresh cranberries

Topping

½ cup all-purpose flour
½ cup old-fashioned oats
½ cup packed brown sugar
¼ teaspoon ground cinnamon
¼ cup butter or margarine, cut into pieces

1 Heat oven to 375°F. Grease bottom and sides of 8-inch square (2-quart) glass baking dish with shortening.

2 In 3-quart saucepan, mix reserved juice from cherries, the granulated sugar, cornstarch and ½ teaspoon cinnamon. Cook over medium heat, stirring constantly, until mixture is bubbly and thickened. Gently stir in cherries, raspberries and cranberries. Spoon into baking dish.

3 In medium bowl, mix all topping ingredients until crumbly; sprinkle over fruit mixture.

4 Bake 30 to 35 minutes or until topping is golden brown and fruit mixture is bubbly.

Crisps and cobblers are best served the same day you make them. The topping can be made a day ahead; just store it in the refrigerator.

1 Serving: Calories 280 (Calories from Fat 60); Total Fat 6g (Saturated Fat 3.5g); Cholesterol 15mg; Sodium 50mg; Total Carbohydrate 54g (Dietary Fiber 4g); Protein 3g

Roasted Almond-Cranberry-Pear Crisp

Prep Time: 25 min ∎ Start to Finish: 1 hr 30 min ∎ 8 Servings

5 cups sliced peeled pears (5 to 6 pears)
2 cups fresh or frozen cranberries
1 cup granulated sugar
3 tablespoons all-purpose flour
6 roasted almond crunchy granola bars (3 pouches from 8.9-oz box),
      finely crushed
½ cup all-purpose flour
¼ cup packed brown sugar
¼ cup butter or margarine, melted
Whipped cream or vanilla ice cream, if desired

1 Heat oven to 350°F. Spray 8-inch square (2-quart) glass baking dish with cooking spray. In large bowl, mix pears, cranberries, granulated sugar and 3 tablespoons flour. Spoon evenly into baking dish.

2 In medium bowl, mix crushed granola bars, ½ cup flour, the brown sugar and butter until crumbly. Sprinkle over pear mixture.

3 Bake 55 to 65 minutes or until top is golden brown and fruit is tender (mixture will be bubbly). Cool slightly. Serve warm or cool with whipped cream or ice cream.

1 Serving: Calories 370 (Calories from Fat 80); Total Fat 9g (Saturated Fat 3g); Cholesterol 15mg; Sodium 100mg; Total Carbohydrate 69g (Dietary Fiber 5g); Protein 3g

You can crush the granola bars right in their pouches or crush them in a food processor.

Two-Berry Crisp with Pecan Streusel Topping

Prep Time: 15 min ▪ Start to Finish: 55 min ▪ 6 Servings

¾ cup quick-cooking oats
½ cup all-purpose flour
½ cup packed brown sugar
½ cup butter or margarine, cut into pieces
¼ cup chopped pecans
1 can (21 oz) blueberry pie filling
2 cups frozen unsweetened raspberries
3 tablespoons granulated sugar
1 tablespoon all-purpose flour

1 Heat oven to 400°F. Spray 8-inch square (2-quart) glass baking dish with cooking spray. In large bowl, mix oats, ½ cup flour and the brown sugar. With fork or pastry blender, cut in butter until mixture is crumbly. Stir in pecans; set aside.

2 In large bowl, mix remaining ingredients. Spread in baking dish. Sprinkle oat mixture over top.

3 Bake 30 to 40 minutes or until fruit mixture is bubbly and topping is golden brown.

Top each serving with whipped cream or ice cream and a few pecan halves.

1 Serving: Calories 490 (Calories from Fat 180); Total Fat 20g (Saturated Fat 8g); Cholesterol 40mg; Sodium 110mg; Total Carbohydrate 74g (Dietary Fiber 9g); Protein 4g

Razzle-Dazzle Berry Shortcake

Prep Time: 10 min ■ Start to Finish: 10 min ■ 6 Servings

1½ cups raspberry pie filling (from 21-oz can)
1 cup sliced fresh strawberries
¾ cup fresh blueberries
6 slices (about ¾ inch thick) angel food or pound cake (3×2½ inches)
¾ cup whipped cream topping in aerosol can

1 In medium bowl, mix pie filling, strawberries and blueberries.

2 Cut each cake slice diagonally in half to make 2 triangles. Arrange 2 triangles on each of 6 serving plates. Top with fruit mixture and whipped cream.

1 Serving: Calories 370 (Calories from Fat 20); Total Fat 2g (Saturated Fat 1g); Cholesterol 5mg; Sodium 310mg; Total Carbohydrate 84g (Dietary Fiber 2g); Protein 4g

Chocolate Mousse

Prep Time: 30 min ■ Start to Finish: 2 hrs 40 min ■ 8 Servings

Mousse
4 egg yolks
¼ cup sugar
1 cup whipping cream
8 oz semisweet baking chocolate,
    chopped
1½ cups whipping cream

Chocolate Piping
½ cup semisweet chocolate chips
½ teaspoon shortening

1 In small bowl, beat egg yolks with electric mixer on high speed about 3 minutes or until thickened and lemon colored. Gradually beat in sugar.

2 In 2-quart saucepan, heat 1 cup of the whipping cream over medium heat just until hot. Gradually stir half of the hot cream into egg yolk mixture, then stir egg mixture back into hot cream in saucepan. Cook over low heat about 5 minutes, stirring constantly, until mixture thickens (do not boil).

3 Stir in baking chocolate until melted. Cover; refrigerate about 2 hours, stirring occasionally, just until chilled.

4 In chilled medium bowl, beat remaining 1½ cups whipping cream on high speed until stiff peaks form. Fold chocolate mixture into whipped cream.

5 In 1-cup microwavable measuring cup, microwave chocolate chips and shortening uncovered on Medium (50%) 30 seconds. Stir; microwave in 10-second increments, stirring after each, until melted and smooth. Place in small resealable food-storage plastic bag; seal bag. Cut off tiny corner of bag. Squeeze bag to pipe designs or swirls inside parfait glasses. Refrigerate 10 minutes to set chocolate.

6 Spoon mousse into decorated glasses. Refrigerate until serving.

1 Serving: Calories 490 (Calories from Fat 330); Total Fat 37g (Saturated Fat 22g); Cholesterol 185mg; Sodium 35mg; Total Carbohydrate 33g (Dietary Fiber 2g); Protein 5g

The cream will whip up faster

if you chill the bowl and beaters in the freezer
for about 15 minutes before whipping.

Easy Tiramisù

Prep Time: 25 min ■ Start to Finish: 2 hrs 10 min ■ 15 Servings

Cake
1 package white cake mix with
    pudding in the mix
1 cup water
⅓ cup vegetable oil
¼ cup brandy
3 egg whites

Espresso Syrup
4 tablespoons instant espresso
    coffee granules

½ cup boiling water
2 tablespoons corn syrup

Topping
1 package (8 oz) cream cheese,
    softened
½ cup powdered sugar
2 cups whipping cream
1 tablespoon unsweetened baking
    cocoa, if desired

1 Heat oven to 350°F. Grease bottom only of 13×9-inch pan with shortening or spray bottom with cooking spray.

2 In large bowl, beat cake mix, 1 cup water, the oil, brandy and egg whites with electric mixer on low speed 30 seconds. Beat on medium speed 2 minutes, scraping bowl occasionally. Pour into pan.

3 Bake 28 to 33 minutes or until toothpick inserted in center comes out clean. Cool 15 minutes.

4 Meanwhile, in small bowl, stir dry espresso granules and ½ cup boiling water until mixed. Stir in corn syrup. Pierce top of cake every ½ inch with long-tined fork. Brush top of cake with espresso syrup. Cool completely, about 1 hour.

5 In medium bowl, beat cream cheese and powdered sugar on low speed until mixed. Beat on high speed until smooth. Gradually beat in whipping cream, beating on high speed about 2 minutes until stiff peaks form. Spread cream mixture over top of cake; dust with baking cocoa. Store loosely covered in refrigerator.

If you prefer, you can use 1½ teaspoons of brandy extract plus ¼ cup water instead of brandy.

1 Serving: Calories 380 (Calories from Fat 220); Total Fat 25g (Saturated Fat 13g); Cholesterol 60mg; Sodium 300mg; Total Carbohydrate 35g (Dietary Fiber 0g); Protein 4g

Fudge Pudding Cake
with Ice Cream

Prep Time: 15 min ▪ Start to Finish: 1 hr 10 min ▪ 9 Servings

1 cup all-purpose flour
¾ cup granulated sugar
2 tablespoons unsweetened baking cocoa
2 teaspoons baking powder
¼ teaspoon salt
½ cup milk
2 tablespoons vegetable oil
1 teaspoon vanilla
1 cup chopped nuts
1 cup packed brown sugar
¼ cup unsweetened baking cocoa
1¾ cups boiling water
4½ cups vanilla ice cream

1 Heat oven to 350°F. In ungreased 9-inch square pan, mix flour, granulated sugar, 2 tablespoons cocoa, the baking powder and salt. Stir in milk, oil and vanilla with fork until smooth. Stir in nuts. Spread evenly in pan.

2 In small bowl, mix brown sugar and ¼ cup cocoa; sprinkle over batter. Pour boiling water over batter.

3 Bake 40 minutes. Let stand 15 minutes. Spoon cake and sauce into individual dishes. Top each serving with ½ cup ice cream.

Serve this delicious dessert with hot coffee or your favorite tea.

1 Serving: Calories 500 (Calories from Fat 180); Total Fat 20g (Saturated Fat 7g); Cholesterol 35mg; Sodium 250mg; Total Carbohydrate 73g (Dietary Fiber 3g); Protein 7g

Crème Brûlée

Prep Time: 20 min ■ Start to Finish: 7 hrs ■ 4 Servings

6 egg yolks	1 teaspoon vanilla
2 cups whipping cream	Boiling water
1/3 cup sugar	8 teaspoons sugar

1 Heat oven to 350°F. In 13×9-inch pan, place 4 (6-oz) ceramic ramekins.* In small bowl, slightly beat egg yolks with wire whisk. In large bowl, stir whipping cream, 1/3 cup sugar and the vanilla until well mixed. Add egg yolks; beat with wire whisk until evenly colored and well blended. Pour cream mixture evenly into ramekins.

2 Carefully place pan with ramekins in oven. Pour enough boiling water into pan, being careful not to splash water into ramekins, until water covers two-thirds of the height of the ramekins.

3 Bake 30 to 40 minutes or until top is light golden brown and sides are set (centers will be jiggly).

4 Using tongs or grasping tops of ramekins with pot holder, carefully transfer ramekins to cooling rack. Cool to room temperature, about 2 hours. Cover tightly with plastic wrap; refrigerate until chilled, at least 4 hours but no longer than 48 hours.

5 Uncover ramekins; gently blot any liquid from tops of custards with paper towel. Sprinkle 2 teaspoons sugar over each chilled custard. Holding kitchen torch 3 to 4 inches from custard, caramelize sugar on each custard by heating with torch about 2 minutes, moving flame continuously over sugar in circular motion, until sugar is melted and light golden brown. (To caramelize sugar in the broiler, see Broiler Directions.) Serve immediately, or refrigerate up to 8 hours before serving.

*Do not use glass custard cups or glass pie plates; they cannot withstand the heat from the kitchen torch or broiler and may break.

1 Serving: Calories 540 (Calories from Fat 390); Total Fat 44g (Saturated Fat 25g); Cholesterol 440mg; Sodium 55mg; Total Carbohydrate 30g (Dietary Fiber 0g); Protein 7g

Broiler Directions:

Sprinkle 2 teaspoons brown sugar over each chilled custard. Place ramekins in 15×10×1-inch pan or on cookie sheet with sides. Broil with tops 4 to 6 inches from heat 5 to 6 minutes or until brown sugar melts and forms a glaze.

Slow Cooker White Chocolate Bread Pudding

Prep Time: 10 min ▪ Start to Finish: 3 hr 40 min ▪ 8 Servings

6 cups French bread cubes
1 package (6 oz) white chocolate baking bar, coarsely chopped
1 cup fat-free egg product
¾ cup warm water
1 teaspoon vanilla
1 can (14 oz) sweetened condensed milk (not evaporated)

1 Spray inside of 3- to 4-quart slow cooker with cooking spray. Place bread cubes in slow cooker. Sprinkle with baking bar.

2 In small bowl, mix remaining ingredients; pour over bread cubes and baking bar.

3 Cover; cook on Low heat setting 3 hours 30 minutes to 4 hours or until toothpick inserted in center comes out clean. Serve warm.

Turn leftover French bread and sweet white chocolate into a rich and satisfying bread pudding dessert. Garnish with fresh raspberries and mint sprigs if desired.

1 Serving: Calories 370 (Calories from Fat 110); Total Fat 12g (Saturated Fat 7g); Cholesterol 20mg; Sodium 290mg; Total Carbohydrate 53g (Dietary Fiber 0g); Protein 11g

Raspberry Bread Pudding

Prep Time: 25 min ∎ Start to Finish: 55 min ∎ 8 Servings

Bread Pudding
6 cups cubed (1-inch cubes) day-old French bread
1 cup fresh raspberries
2 tablespoons miniature semisweet chocolate chips
2 cups fat-free (skim) milk
½ cup fat-free egg product
¼ cup packed brown sugar
1 teaspoon vanilla
Sauce
½ cup granulated sugar
2 tablespoons cornstarch
¾ cup water
1 bag (12 oz) frozen unsweetened raspberries, thawed, undrained

1 Heat oven to 350°F. Spray bottom and sides of 8-inch square (2-quart) glass baking dish with cooking spray. In large bowl, place bread, 1 cup raspberries and chocolate chips.

2 In medium bowl, mix milk, egg product, brown sugar and vanilla with wire whisk or fork until blended. Pour egg mixture over bread mixture; stir gently until bread is coated. Spread in baking dish.

3 Bake 40 to 50 minutes or until golden brown and set.

4 Meanwhile, in 2-quart saucepan, mix granulated sugar and cornstarch. Stir in water and thawed raspberries. Heat to boiling over medium heat, stirring constantly and pressing raspberries to release juice. Boil about 1 minute or until thick. Place small strainer over small bowl. Pour mixture through strainer to remove seeds; discard seeds. Serve sauce with warm bread pudding.

1 Serving: Calories 230 (Calories from Fat 20); Total Fat 2g (Saturated Fat 1g); Cholesterol 0mg; Sodium 210mg; Total Carbohydrate 46g (Dietary Fiber 5g); Protein 7g

Chocolate-Strawberry-Walnut Crumble Dessert

Prep Time: 15 min ■ Start to Finish: 1 hr 30 min ■ 16 Servings

2 cans (21 oz each) strawberry pie filling
1 box (10 oz) frozen strawberries in syrup, thawed
1 package devil's food cake mix with pudding in the mix
¾ cup butter or margarine, softened
½ cup chopped walnuts
Vanilla ice cream, if desired

1 Heat oven to 350°F (325°F for dark or nonstick pan). In ungreased 13×9-inch pan, pour pie filling and strawberries; stir gently to mix.

2 In large bowl, beat cake mix and butter with electric mixer on low speed until crumbly. Crumble over fruit mixture. Sprinkle with walnuts.

3 Bake 40 to 45 minutes or until bubbly around edges and top is set. Cool at least 30 minutes. Serve warm with ice cream.

For mixed-berry crumble, use a can of raspberry pie filling in place of one of the cans of strawberry filling.

1 Serving: Calories 330 (Calories from Fat 120); Total Fat 13g (Saturated Fat 7g); Cholesterol 25mg; Sodium 320mg; Total Carbohydrate 49g (Dietary Fiber 2g); Protein 2g

Light 'n' Creamy Tropical Dessert

Prep Time: 15 min ■ Start to Finish: 5 hrs ■ 15 Servings

Almond Crust
1½ cups all-purpose flour
1 cup butter or margarine, softened
½ cup powdered sugar
½ cup finely chopped slivered almonds

Dessert
1 package (8 oz) cream cheese, softened
⅔ cup granulated sugar

1 teaspoon vanilla
1 can (20 oz) pineapple tidbits in juice, drained, 1 cup juice reserved
1½ cups whipping cream
2 cups miniature marshmallows
1 tablespoon cornstarch
1 papaya or mango, peeled, seeded and cut into pieces
1 kiwifruit, peeled, cut into pieces

1 Heat oven to 400°F. In large bowl, beat flour, butter and powdered sugar with electric mixer on low speed 1 minute, scraping bowl constantly. Beat on high speed about 2 minutes or until creamy. Stir in almonds. Press mixture evenly in bottom of ungreased 13×9-inch pan. Bake 12 to 15 minutes or until edges are golden brown. Cool completely, about 30 minutes.

2 In large bowl, mix cream cheese, granulated sugar and vanilla with spoon. Reserve ½ cup of the pineapple. Stir remaining pineapple into cream cheese mixture.

3 In chilled medium bowl, beat whipping cream with electric mixer on high speed until stiff peaks form. Fold whipped cream and marshmallows into cream cheese mixture. Spread over crust. Cover and refrigerate at least 4 hours until set but no longer than 48 hours.

4 In 1-quart saucepan, place cornstarch. Gradually stir in reserved 1 cup pineapple juice. Cook over medium heat, stirring constantly, until thickened and bubbly. Cook and stir 2 minutes longer. Cool completely, about 30 minutes. Fold in reserved ½ cup pineapple, the papaya and kiwifruit. Cut dessert into 5 rows by 3 rows. Serve with fruit mixture. Store covered in refrigerator.

You can find already sliced pieces of papaya and mango or a mixture of tropical fruits packed in jars in the produce section of the supermarket. To use, cut up if necessary and drain before adding to the cornstarch mixture.

1 Serving: Calories 420 (Calories from Fat 260); Total Fat 28g (Saturated Fat 15g); Cholesterol 80mg; Sodium 140mg; Total Carbohydrate 39g (Dietary Fiber 2g); Protein 4g

Chocolate Mousse Brownie Dessert

Prep Time: 15 min ∎ Start to Finish: 2 hrs 20 min ∎ 12 to 16 Servings

1 package brownie mix (with chocolate syrup pouch)
⅓ cup water
⅓ cup vegetable oil
2 eggs
¾ cup whipping cream
1 cup semisweet chocolate chips (6 oz)
3 eggs
⅓ cup sugar

1 Heat oven to 350°F. Grease bottom only of 10-inch springform pan with shortening. Make brownie mix as directed on package, using water, oil and 2 eggs. Spread in pan.

2 In 2-quart saucepan, heat whipping cream and chocolate chips over medium heat, stirring constantly, until chocolate is melted and mixture is smooth; cool slightly.

3 In small bowl, beat 3 eggs and sugar with electric mixer on medium speed until foamy; stir into chocolate mixture. Pour evenly over batter.

4 Bake about 1 hour 5 minutes or until topping is set. Cool completely, about 1 hour. Run metal spatula around side of dessert to loosen; remove side of pan. Serve at room temperature, or cover tightly and refrigerate until chilled.

Top with whipped cream and, if desired, chocolate decorations or shavings.

1 Serving: Calories 440 (Calories from Fat 180); Total Fat 20g (Saturated Fat 8g); Cholesterol 105mg; Sodium 210mg; Total Carbohydrate 60g (Dietary Fiber 2g); Protein 5g

Rich Peanut Butter Cookies

White Chocolate Chunk–Macadamia Cookies

Apricot Spice Cookies

Crunchy Muncher Cookies

Trail Mix Cookies

Rainbow Sprinklers

Citrus Shortbread Cookies

Fudge Crinkles

Triple-Ginger Bars

Lemon Squares

Caramel Brownies

White Chocolate Chunk Blonde Brownies

Brownie Pops

Rocky Road Bars

Salted Nut Bars

Chewy Peanut Bars

Double-Chocolate Candy Cashew Bars

Toffee Bars

Cinnamon Espresso Bars

Confetti Caramel Bars

Tropical Fruit Bars

Carrot-Raisin Bars

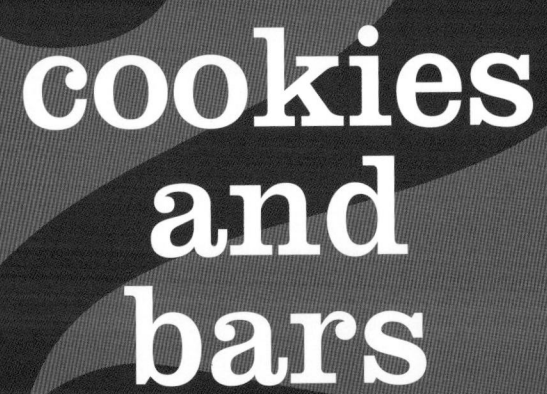

2

cookies
and
bars

Rich Peanut Butter Cookies

Prep Time: 40 min ■ Start to Finish: 40 min ■ About 2 Dozen Cookies

1 cup packed brown sugar
½ cup peanut butter
½ cup butter or margarine, softened
1 egg
1¼ cups all-purpose flour
¾ teaspoon baking soda
½ teaspoon baking powder
¼ teaspoon salt
1 cup peanut butter chips
Granulated sugar

1 Heat oven to 375°F. In large bowl, beat brown sugar, peanut butter, butter and egg with electric mixer on medium speed until creamy, or mix with spoon. Stir in flour, baking soda, baking powder and salt. Stir in peanut butter chips.

2 Shape dough into 1½-inch balls. Dip tops of balls into granulated sugar. On ungreased cookie sheet, place balls, sugared sides up, about 3 inches apart (do not flatten).

3 Bake 9 to 10 minutes or until light brown. Cool 5 minutes; remove from cookie sheet to wire rack.

1 Cookie: Calories 170 (Calories from Fat 80); Total Fat 9g (Saturated Fat 3g); Cholesterol 20mg; Sodium 150mg; Total Carbohydrate 19g (Dietary Fiber 0g); Protein 3g

For the best results, always place cookie dough on a cool cookie sheet. This will help prevent spreading during baking.

White Chocolate Chunk–Macadamia Cookies

Prep Time: 1 hr ■ Start to Finish: 1 hr ■ About 2½ Dozen Cookies

1 cup packed brown sugar
½ cup granulated sugar
½ cup butter or margarine, softened
½ cup shortening
1 teaspoon vanilla
1 egg
2¼ cups all-purpose flour
1 teaspoon baking soda
¼ teaspoon salt
1 package (6 oz) Swiss confectionery bars (white chocolate), cut into ¼- to ½-inch chunks
1 jar (3.25 oz) macadamia nuts, coarsely chopped

1 Heat oven to 350°F. In large bowl, beat sugars, butter, shortening, vanilla and egg with electric mixer on medium speed until light and fluffy, or mix with spoon. Stir in flour, baking soda and salt (dough will be stiff). Stir in baking bar chunks and nuts.

2 On ungreased cookie sheet, drop dough by rounded tablespoonfuls about 2 inches apart.

3 Bake 11 to 13 minutes or until light brown. Cool 1 to 2 minutes; remove from cookie sheet to wire rack.

If you don't have macadamia nuts, use walnuts or pecans instead.

1 Cookie: Calories 190 (Calories from Fat 100); Total Fat 11g (Saturated Fat 4g); Cholesterol 15mg; Sodium 100mg; Total Carbohydrate 21g (Dietary Fiber 0g); Protein 2g

Apricot Spice Cookies

Prep Time: 1 hr 20 min ▪ Start to Finish: 1 hr 20 min ▪ About 6 Dozen Cookies

⅔ cup granulated sugar
⅔ cup packed brown sugar
½ cup butter or margarine, softened
½ cup shortening
1 teaspoon baking soda
1 teaspoon ground cinnamon or cardamom
1 teaspoon vanilla
½ teaspoon baking powder
½ teaspoon salt
2 eggs
3 cups quick-cooking oats
1 cup all-purpose flour
¾ cup chopped dried apricots
½ cup finely chopped pecans

1 Heat oven to 375°F. In large bowl, beat all ingredients except oats, flour, apricots and pecans with electric mixer on medium speed until creamy, or mix with spoon. Stir in remaining ingredients.

2 On ungreased cookie sheet, drop dough by rounded teaspoonfuls about 2 inches apart.

3 Bake 8 to 10 minutes or until edges are brown and centers are soft. Cool 1 to 2 minutes; remove from cookie sheet to wire rack.

To make drop cookies uniform in size, use a spring-handled cookie scoop, available in a variety of sizes at most grocery and discount stores.

1 Cookie: Calories 70 (Calories from Fat 35); Total Fat 3.5g (Saturated Fat 1g); Cholesterol 10mg; Sodium 50mg; Total Carbohydrate 8g (Dietary Fiber 0g); Protein 1g

Crunchy Muncher Cookies

Prep Time: 2 hrs 10 min ■ Start to Finish: 2 hrs 10 min ■ About 9 Dozen Cookies

1 cup granulated sugar
1 cup packed brown sugar
1 cup butter or margarine, softened
²⁄₃ cup vegetable oil
1 teaspoon vanilla
3 eggs
3½ cups all-purpose flour
1 teaspoon baking soda
1 teaspoon cream of tartar
¼ teaspoon salt
2²⁄₃ cups small pretzel twists, coarsely crushed
1 cup old-fashioned or quick-cooking oats
1 cup Wheaties® cereal, slightly crushed
1 cup miniature semisweet chocolate chips
1 cup butterscotch-flavored chips

1 Heat oven to 350°F. In large bowl, beat sugars, butter, oil, vanilla and eggs with electric mixer on medium speed until light and fluffy, or mix with spoon. Stir in flour, baking soda, cream of tartar and salt. Stir in remaining ingredients.

2 On ungreased cookie sheet, drop dough by heaping teaspoonfuls about 2 inches apart.

3 Bake 9 to 11 minutes or until light brown. Cool 1 minute; remove from cookie sheet to wire rack.

Vary the flavor of chips used in these cookies. Use all chocolate or all butterscotch, or add some peanut butter or white baking chips.

1 Cookie: Calories 80 (Calories from Fat 40); Total Fat 4.5g (Saturated Fat 2g); Cholesterol 10mg; Sodium 60mg; Total Carbohydrate 11g (Dietary Fiber 0g); Protein 0g

Trail Mix Cookies

Prep Time: 1 hr 10 min ▪ Start to Finish: 1 hr 10 min ▪ About 5 Dozen Cookies

1 cup granulated sugar
1 cup packed brown sugar
1 cup peanut butter
½ cup butter or margarine, softened
½ cup shortening
2 teaspoons vanilla
2 eggs
2 cups all-purpose flour
1½ cups old-fashioned or quick-cooking oats
1 teaspoon baking powder
1 teaspoon baking soda
2 cups candy-coated chocolate candies
1 cup peanuts
¾ cup raisins

1 Heat oven to 375°F. In large bowl, beat sugars, peanut butter, butter, shortening, vanilla and eggs with electric mixer on medium speed until creamy, or mix with spoon. Stir in flour, oats, baking powder and baking soda thoroughly. Stir in candies, peanuts and raisins.

2 On ungreased cookie sheet, drop dough by rounded tablespoonfuls about 2 inches apart; flatten slightly with fork.

3 Bake 9 to 10 minutes or until light brown. Cool 1 minute; remove from cookie sheet to wire rack.

Tailor these cookies to suit your taste. You could omit the peanuts and increase the raisins, or substitute walnuts for the peanuts.

1 Cookie: Calories 160 (Calories from Fat 80); Total Fat 8g (Saturated Fat 3g); Cholesterol 10mg; Sodium 80mg; Total Carbohydrate 19g (Dietary Fiber 1g); Protein 3g

Rainbow Sprinklers

Prep Time: 1 hr 15 min ■ Start to Finish: 1 hr 15 min ■ About 6 Dozen Cookies

1½ cups granulated sugar
½ cup butter or margarine, softened
½ cup shortening
2 eggs
2¾ cups all-purpose flour
2 teaspoons cream of tartar
1 teaspoon baking soda
¼ teaspoon salt
About 1½ cups assorted colored sugars or candy decors

1 Heat oven to 400°F. In large bowl, stir sugar, butter, shortening and eggs with spoon until mixed. Stir in flour, cream of tartar, baking soda and salt.

2 Shape dough by rounded teaspoonfuls into balls. Roll balls in colored sugar until coated. On ungreased cookie sheet, place balls about 2 inches apart.

3 Bake 8 to 10 minutes or until centers are almost set. Cool 1 minute; remove from cookie sheet to wire rack.

1 Cookie: Calories 80 (Calories from Fat 25); Total Fat 3g (Saturated Fat 1g); Cholesterol 10mg; Sodium 35mg; Total Carbohydrate 12g (Dietary Fiber 0g); Protein 0g

Citrus Shortbread Cookies

Prep Time: 15 min ■ Start to Finish: 50 min ■ 24 Cookies

¾ cup butter or margarine, softened
¼ cup granulated sugar
2 cups all-purpose flour
1½ teaspoons grated lime peel
1½ teaspoons grated orange peel
1 cup powdered sugar
1 to 2 tablespoons lime juice

1 Heat oven to 350°F. In large bowl, beat butter and granulated sugar with electric mixer on medium speed 2 to 3 minutes or until light and creamy. Add flour, lime peel and orange peel. Beat on low speed until mixture is blended. Gather dough into a ball.

2 On lightly floured surface, roll dough into 8×6-inch rectangle, about ½ inch thick. (If dough cracks around edges, press edges together to smooth.) Cut into 12 (2-inch) squares, then cut each square diagonally in half into triangles. On ungreased cookie sheet, place triangles ½ inch apart.

3 Bake 12 to 17 minutes or until edges just begin to brown. Cool 1 minute; remove from cookie sheet to wire rack. Cool completely, about 15 minutes.

4 In small bowl, mix powdered sugar and lime juice with spoon until smooth and thin enough to drizzle. Drizzle glaze over cookies.

For easy glazing, put powdered sugar mixture into quart-size plastic food-storage bag. Snip off a tiny piece of one corner with kitchen scissors and squeeze to drizzle glaze over shortbread.

1 Cookie: Calories 120 (Calories from Fat 50); Total Fat 6g (Saturated Fat 3.5g); Cholesterol 15mg; Sodium 40mg; Total Carbohydrate 15g (Dietary Fiber 0g); Protein 1g

Fudge Crinkles

Prep Time: 1 hr ■ Start to Finish: 1 hr ■ 30 Cookies

1 package devil's food cake mix with pudding in the mix
½ cup vegetable oil
2 eggs
1 teaspoon vanilla
⅓ cup powdered sugar

1 Heat oven to 350°F. In large bowl, mix cake mix, oil, eggs and vanilla with spoon until dough forms.

2 Shape dough into 1-inch balls. Roll balls in powdered sugar. On ungreased cookie sheet, place balls about 2 inches apart.

3 Bake 10 to 12 minutes or until set. Cool 1 minute; remove from cookie sheet to cooling rack. Cool completely, about 30 minutes. Store tightly covered.

For extra fun, stir 1 cup mini candy-coated chocolate baking bits into the dough.

1 Cookie: Calories 110 (Calories from Fat 45); Total Fat 5g (Saturated Fat 1g); Cholesterol 15mg; Sodium 140mg; Total Carbohydrate 15g (Dietary Fiber 0g); Protein 1g

Triple-Ginger Bars

Prep Time: 20 min ▪ Start to Finish: 2 hrs 45 min ▪ 2 Dozen Bars

1 package white cake mix with pudding in the mix
½ cup butter or margarine, melted
2 eggs
¼ cup finely chopped crystallized ginger
1 tablespoon grated gingerroot
1 teaspoon ground ginger
2 tablespoons decorator sugar crystals

1 Heat oven to 350°F. Grease bottom only of rectangular pan, 13×9×2 inches, with shortening or spray with cooking spray.

2 In large bowl, mix cake mix, butter and eggs in large bowl with spoon until well blended. Stir in remaining ingredients except sugar. Press dough evenly in pan with greased fingers. Sprinkle with sugar.

3 Bake 18 to 23 minutes or until edges are very light golden brown. Cool completely, about 2 hours. Cut into 6 rows by 4 rows.

1 Bar: Calories 140 (Calories from Fat 60); Total Fat 6g (Saturated Fat 2.5g); Cholesterol 30mg; Sodium 180mg; Total Carbohydrate 20g (Dietary Fiber 0g); Protein 1g

Crystallized or candied ginger is gingerroot that has been cooked in sugar syrup and coated with coarse sugar. It feels dry to the touch but is sticky when chopped. In the supermarket, it can be packaged in a plastic bag in the specialty produce section or found in glass jars in the spice aisle.

Lemon Squares

Prep Time: 25 min ▪ Start to Finish: 2 hrs 15 min ▪ 25 Squares

1 cup all-purpose flour
½ cup butter or margarine, softened
¼ cup powdered sugar
1 cup granulated sugar
2 teaspoons grated lemon peel, if desired
2 tablespoons lemon juice
½ teaspoon baking powder
¼ teaspoon salt
2 eggs
Additional powdered sugar

1 Heat oven to 350°F. In small bowl, mix flour, butter and ¼ cup powdered sugar. Press mixture in bottom of ungreased 8-inch or 9-inch square pan, building up ½-inch edge. Bake 20 minutes.

2 Meanwhile, in small bowl, beat granulated sugar, lemon peel, lemon juice, baking powder, salt and eggs with electric mixer on high speed about 3 minutes or until light and fluffy. Pour over hot crust.

3 Bake 25 to 30 minutes or until almost no indentation remains when touched lightly in center. Cool completely, about 1 hour. Sprinkle with additional powdered sugar. Cut into 5 rows by 5 rows.

1 Square: Calories 90 (Calories from Fat 35); Total Fat 4g (Saturated Fat 2g); Cholesterol 25mg; Sodium 65mg; Total Carbohydrate 13g (Dietary Fiber 0g); Protein 1g

Caramel Brownies

Prep Time: 30 min ▪ Start to Finish: 3 hrs 10 min ▪ 32 Brownies

1 bag (14 oz) caramels, unwrapped
¼ cup milk
1 package brownie mix (with chocolate syrup pouch)
Water, oil and eggs called for on brownie mix package directions
1 cup semisweet chocolate chips (6 oz)
1 cup coarsely chopped nuts

1 Heat oven to 350°F. Grease bottom only of 13×9-inch pan with shortening or cooking spray. In 1½-quart saucepan, heat caramels and milk over medium-low heat, stirring frequently, until melted and smooth.

2 In medium bowl, stir brownie mix, chocolate syrup, water, oil and eggs until well blended. Spread in pan. Drizzle caramel mixture evenly over batter. Sprinkle with chocolate chips and nuts.

3 Bake 35 to 40 minutes or until edges are set. Cool completely, about 2 hours. Cut into 8 rows by 4 rows. Store covered at room temperature.

For super-easy cleanup, line your baking pan with foil that is longer than the pan. Spray the bottom of the foil as directed. When brownies are cool, lift them out of the pan by the foil "handles," peel back foil and cut.

1 Brownie: Calories 210 (Calories from Fat 80); Total Fat 9g (Saturated Fat 2.5g); Cholesterol 15mg; Sodium 100mg; Total Carbohydrate 30g (Dietary Fiber 1g); Protein 2g

White Chocolate Chunk Blonde Brownies

Prep Time: 20 min ▪ Start to Finish: 2 hrs 55 min ▪ 36 Brownies

2 cups packed brown sugar
½ cup butter or margarine, softened
2 teaspoons vanilla
½ teaspoon rum extract
2 eggs
2 cups all-purpose flour
1 teaspoon baking powder
¼ teaspoon salt
1 bag (12 oz) white chocolate chunks
1 cup chopped walnuts
¼ cup semisweet chocolate chunks (from 12-oz bag)
1 teaspoon vegetable oil

1 Heat oven to 350°F. In large bowl, beat brown sugar, butter, vanilla, rum extract and eggs with electric mixer on medium speed until light and fluffy.

2 Beat in flour, baking powder and salt on low speed until well blended. Stir in white chocolate chunks and walnuts. In ungreased 13×9-inch pan, spread batter evenly.

3 Bake 25 to 35 minutes or until top is golden brown and set. Cool completely, about 2 hours.

4 In small microwavable bowl, microwave semisweet chocolate chunks and oil uncovered on High 30 to 60 seconds, stirring every 15 seconds, until melted; stir well. Spread chocolate glaze over brownies. If desired, place glaze in small reasealable plastic food storage bag and snip off a tiny corner with kitchen scissors. Drizzle glaze in diagonal lines over brownies. Let stand until glaze is set. Cut into 6 rows by 6 rows.

1 Brownie: Calories 180 (Calories from Fat 80); Total Fat 9g (Saturated Fat 3.5g); Cholesterol 20mg; Sodium 65mg; Total Carbohydrate 24g (Dietary Fiber 0g); Protein 2g

Brownie Pops

Prep Time: 30 min ■ Start to Finish: 2 hrs 30 min ■ 24 Pops

1 package (1 lb 6.5 oz) brownie mix (with chocolate syrup pouch)
Water, vegetable oil and eggs called for on brownie mix package directions
24 craft sticks (flat wooden sticks with round ends)
1 cup semisweet chocolate chips (6 oz)
2 teaspoons shortening
Assorted decors or sprinkles

1 Heat oven to 350°F. Line 13×9-inch pan with foil so foil extends about 2 inches over sides of pan. Spray foil with cooking spray. Make brownie mix as directed on package for 13×9-inch pan. Cool completely, about 1 hour.

2 Place brownies in freezer for 30 minutes. Remove brownies from pan by lifting foil; peel foil from sides of brownies. Cut brownies into 24 rectangular bars, 6 strips lengthwise and 4 rows across, each about 1½ by 3¼ inches. Gently insert stick into end of each bar, peeling foil from bars. Place on baking sheet; freeze 30 minutes.

3 In small microwavable bowl, microwave chocolate chips and shortening uncovered on High about 1 minute; stir until smooth. If necessary, microwave additional 5 seconds at a time. Dip top ⅓ to ½ of each brownie into chocolate; sprinkle with decors. Lay flat on waxed paper or foil to dry.

Visit a cake decorating–supply store or website to find an array of candy sprinkles.

1 Pop: Calories 180 (Calories from Fat 70); Total Fat 7g (Saturated Fat 2.5g); Cholesterol 20mg; Sodium 95mg; Total Carbohydrate 28g (Dietary Fiber 1g); Protein 2g

Rocky Road Bars

Prep Time: 15 min ■ Start to Finish: 1 hr 50 min ■ 24 Bars

1 package chocolate fudge or devil's food cake mix with pudding in the mix
½ cup butter or margarine, melted
⅓ cup water
¼ cup packed brown sugar
2 eggs
1 cup chopped nuts
3 cups miniature marshmallows
½ cup pastel colored candy-coated chocolate candies, if desired
⅓ cup chocolate frosting (from 1-lb container)

1 Heat oven to 350°F (325°F for dark or nonstick pan). Spray bottom and sides of 13×9-inch pan with baking spray with flour.

2 In large bowl, mix half of the cake mix, the butter, water, brown sugar and eggs with spoon until smooth. Stir in remaining cake mix and the nuts. Spread in pan.

3 Bake 20 minutes (25 minutes for dark or nonstick pan); sprinkle with marshmallows. Bake 10 to 15 minutes longer (14 to 18 minutes for dark or nonstick pan) or until marshmallows are puffed and golden. Sprinkle with candies.

4 In small microwavable bowl, microwave frosting uncovered on High 15 seconds; drizzle over bars. Cool completely, about 1 hour. For easier cutting, use plastic knife dipped in hot water. Cut into 6 rows by 4 rows. Store covered.

You can use any kind of nuts, but peanuts are classic in Rocky Road recipes.

1 Bar: Calories 210 (Calories from Fat 90); Total Fat 10g (Saturated Fat 3.5g); Cholesterol 30mg; Sodium 220mg; Total Carbohydrate 28g (Dietary Fiber 0g); Protein 2g

Salted Nut Bars

Prep Time: 30 min ∎ Start to Finish: 50 min ∎ 32 Bars

1½ cups all-purpose flour
¾ cup packed brown sugar
¼ teaspoon salt
½ cup butter or margarine, softened
2 cups salted mixed nuts or peanuts
1 cup butterscotch-flavored chips
½ cup light corn syrup
2 tablespoons butter or margarine

1 Heat oven to 350°F. In medium bowl, mix flour, brown sugar and salt. With fork or pastry blender, cut in ½ cup butter until evenly mixed. Press mixture evenly in bottom of ungreased 13×9-inch pan. Bake 15 minutes.

2 Cut up any large nuts. Sprinkle nuts evenly over crust. In 1-quart saucepan, heat remaining ingredients over low heat, stirring occasionally, just until chips are melted.

3 Drizzle butterscotch mixture evenly over nuts. Bake 5 minutes. Cut into 8 rows by 4 rows while warm for easiest cutting.

These bars are perfect to wrap individually and pack in lunch boxes.

1 Bar: Calories 170 (Calories from Fat 90); Total Fat 10g (Saturated Fat 4g); Cholesterol 10mg; Sodium 115mg; Total Carbohydrate 19g (Dietary Fiber 0g); Protein 2g

Chewy Peanut Bars

Prep Time: 20 min ▮ Start to Finish: 50 min ▮ 24 Bars

4 cups Wheaties cereal
⅓ cup salted dry-roasted peanuts, coarsely chopped
½ cup light corn syrup
⅓ cup packed brown sugar
¼ cup peanut butter
3 tablespoons semisweet chocolate chips

1 Spray 9-inch square pan with cooking spray. In large bowl, mix cereal and peanuts.

2 In 2-quart saucepan, heat corn syrup, brown sugar and peanut butter to boiling over medium heat, stirring constantly. Boil and stir 1 minute. Pour over cereal mixture, stirring to coat entire mixture. Press mixture evenly in pan.

3 In small microwavable bowl, microwave chocolate chips uncovered on High 30 seconds; stir. Continue microwaving 10 seconds at a time, stirring after each microwave time, until smooth. Drizzle chocolate over bars. Refrigerate about 30 minutes or until chocolate has hardened. Cut into 6 rows by 4 rows.

1 Bar: Calories 90 (Calories from Fat 25); Total Fat 3g (Saturated Fat 0.5g); Cholesterol 0mg; Sodium 75mg; Total Carbohydrate 14g (Dietary Fiber 0g); Protein 2g

Double-Chocolate Candy Cashew Bars

Prep Time: 10 min ■ Start to Finish: 2 hrs 45 min ■ 36 Bars

1 package (18 oz) refrigerated chocolate chunk cookie dough
1 cup white vanilla baking chips
1½ cups cashew halves and pieces
½ cup caramel topping
1 tablespoon all-purpose flour
½ cup miniature candy-coated milk chocolate baking bits

1 Heat oven to 350°F. Spray bottom and sides of 13×9-inch pan with cooking spray. Cut cookie dough into ½-inch slices. Arrange slices in bottom of pan. Press dough evenly to form crust. Bake 10 to 15 minutes or until light golden brown.

2 Sprinkle white baking chips and cashews over warm crust. In small bowl, mix caramel topping and flour until smooth; drizzle over baking chips and cashews. Sprinkle with milk chocolate baking bits; press lightly.

3 Bake 15 to 20 minutes or until topping is bubbly. Cool completely, 1 hour 30 minutes to 2 hours, before cutting. Cut into 6 rows by 6 rows.

1 Bar: Calories 170 (Calories from Fat 80); Total Fat 9g (Saturated Fat 3.5g); Cholesterol 0mg; Sodium 70mg; Total Carbohydrate 20g (Dietary Fiber 0g); Protein 2g

Toffee Bars

Prep Time: 15 min ▪ Start to Finish: 1 hr 15 min ▪ 32 Bars

1 cup butter or margarine, softened
1 cup packed brown sugar
1 teaspoon vanilla
1 egg yolk
2 cups all-purpose flour
¼ teaspoon salt
⅔ cup milk chocolate chips
½ cup chopped nuts, if desired

1 Heat oven to 350°F. In large bowl, mix butter, brown sugar, vanilla and egg yolk. Stir in flour and salt. Press mixture evenly in bottom of ungreased 13×9-inch pan.

2 Bake 25 to 30 minutes or until very light brown (crust will be soft). Immediately sprinkle chocolate chips on hot crust. Let stand about 5 minutes or until chocolate is soft; spread evenly. Sprinkle with nuts.

3 Cool 30 minutes in pan on wire rack. Cut into 8 rows by 4 rows.

Cut the bars while they're still warm—your knife will glide through very easily.

1 Bar: Calories 130 (Calories from Fat 60); Total Fat 7g (Saturated Fat 3.5g); Cholesterol 25mg; Sodium 65mg; Total Carbohydrate 15g (Dietary Fiber 0g); Protein 1g

Cinnamon Espresso Bars

Prep Time: 15 min ∎ Start to Finish: 35 min ∎ 48 Bars

Bars
1 cup packed brown sugar
⅓ cup butter or margarine, softened
1 egg
1½ cups all-purpose flour
1 tablespoon instant espresso
    coffee granules
1 teaspoon baking powder
½ teaspoon ground cinnamon
¼ teaspoon salt

¼ teaspoon baking soda
½ cup water

Cinnamon Espresso Glaze
1 cup powdered sugar
¼ teaspoon vanilla
⅛ teaspoon ground cinnamon
4 to 5 teaspoons cold espresso
    coffee or strong coffee

1 Heat oven to 350°F. Grease bottom and sides of 13×9-inch pan with shortening or spray with cooking spray; coat with flour. In large bowl, beat brown sugar, butter and egg with electric mixer on medium speed until blended, or mix with spoon. Stir in remaining bar ingredients. Spread in pan.

2 Bake 20 to 22 minutes or until top springs back when touched in center.

3 Meanwhile, in small bowl, mix all glaze ingredients with spoon until smooth and thin enough to drizzle. Drizzle over bars while warm. Cool completely, about 1 hour. Cut into 8 rows by 6 rows.

Espresso gives these bars a rich coffee flavor, but if you don't have it on hand, you could use regular instant coffee granules for a milder flavor.

1 Bar: Calories 50 (Calories from Fat 15); Total Fat 1.5g (Saturated Fat 0.5g); Cholesterol 10mg; Sodium 40mg; Total Carbohydrate 10g (Dietary Fiber 0g); Protein 0g

Confetti Caramel Bars

Prep Time: 30 min ∎ Start to Finish: 3 hrs 30 min ∎ 32 Bars

1 cup packed brown sugar
1 cup butter or margarine, softened
1½ teaspoons vanilla
1 egg
2 cups all-purpose flour
½ cup light corn syrup
2 tablespoons butter or margarine
1 cup butterscotch-flavored chips
1½ to 2 cups assorted candies and nuts (such as candy corn, candy-coated
   chocolate candies and salted peanuts)

1 Heat oven to 350°F. In large bowl, beat brown sugar, 1 cup butter, vanilla and egg with electric mixer on medium speed, or mix with spoon. Stir in flour. Press mixture evenly in bottom of ungreased 13x9-inch pan. Bake 20 to 22 minutes or until light brown. Cool 20 minutes.

2 Meanwhile, in 1-quart saucepan, heat corn syrup, 2 tablespoons butter and butterscotch chips over medium heat, stirring occasionally, until chips are melted; remove from heat. Cool 10 minutes.

3 Spread butterscotch mixture over crust. Sprinkle with candies and nuts; gently press into butterscotch mixture. Cover and refrigerate at least 2 hours until butterscotch mixture is firm. Cut into 8 rows by 4 rows, or cut into triangle shapes.

1 Bar: Calories 210 (Calories from Fat 90); Total Fat 10g (Saturated Fat 5g); Cholesterol 25mg; Sodium 80mg; Total Carbohydrate 27g (Dietary Fiber 0g); Protein 2g

Tropical Fruit Bars

Prep Time: 20 min ▪ Start to Finish: 3 hrs ▪ 32 Bars

1 package yellow cake mix with pudding in the mix
½ cup butter or margarine, melted
1 egg
1½ cups white vanilla baking chips
1 bag (7 oz) dried tropical fruit mix
1 cup flaked coconut
1 cup cashew pieces
1 can (14 oz) sweetened condensed milk (not evaporated)

1 Heat oven to 350°F (325°F for dark or nonstick pan). Spray bottom and sides of 13×9-inch pan with baking spray with flour.

2 In medium bowl, stir cake mix, butter and egg until mixed. Press mixture evenly in bottom of pan. Sprinkle evenly with baking chips, dried fruit, coconut and cashews. Pour milk evenly over top.

3 Bake 35 to 40 minutes or until edges and center are golden brown. Cool completely, about 2 hours. Cut into 8 rows by 4 rows.

These bars are rich and chewy but not messy. They are perfect to tote to a family picnic.

1 Bar: Calories 240 (Calories from Fat 100); Total Fat 11g (Saturated Fat 6g); Cholesterol 20mg; Sodium 170mg; Total Carbohydrate 33g (Dietary Fiber 0g); Protein 3g

Carrot-Raisin Bars

Prep Time: 10 min ■ Start to Finish: 1 hr 40 min ■ 48 Bars

1 package carrot cake mix with pudding in the mix
½ cup vegetable oil
¼ cup water
2 eggs
¾ cup raisins
½ cup chopped nuts
1 container (1 lb) cream cheese frosting

1 Heat oven to 350°F (325°F for dark or nonstick pan). Spray bottom and sides of 15×10×1-inch pan with baking spray with flour.

2 In large bowl, mix cake mix, oil, water and eggs with spoon until mixed. Stir in raisins and nuts. Spread mixture evenly in pan.

3 Bake 18 to 24 minutes (25 to 29 minutes for dark or nonstick pan) or until bars spring back when touched lightly in center. Cool completely, about 1 hour.

4 Spread with frosting. Cut into 8 rows by 6 rows. Store loosely covered at room temperature.

1 Bar: Calories 120 (Calories from Fat 50); Total Fat 6g (Saturated Fat 1.5g); Cholesterol 10mg; Sodium 90mg; Total Carbohydrate 16g (Dietary Fiber 0g); Protein 0g

For a hint of orange flavor, substitute orange juice for the water. You can also stir a little grated orange peel into the frosting.

Chocolate Lover's Dream Cake

Triple-Fudge Cake

Cinnamon Streusel Coffee Cake

Lemon–Poppy Seed Bundt Cake

Caramel-Carrot Cake

Margarita Cake

Dulce de Leche Cake

Luscious Mandarin Orange Cake

Lemon-Raspberry Cake

Lemon Mousse Cake

Almond-Orange Cake,

Watermelon Slices Cake

Caramel Cappuccino Cheesecake

Strawberry-Filled Cheesecake

Mango-Strawberry Sorbet Torte

Double Chocolate–Cherry Torte

Triple-Chocolate Torte

Strawberry–Cream Cheese Cupcakes

Chocolate Chip Cheesecake Swirl Cupcakes

Key West Cupcakes

Molten Chocolate Cupcakes

Chocolate Cupcakes with White Truffle Frosting

Frosted Cupcake Cones

3

cakes
and
cupcakes

Chocolate Lover's Dream Cake

Prep Time: 20 min ∎ Start to Finish: 3 hrs 35 min ∎ 16 Servings

Cake

1 package butter recipe chocolate
    cake mix with pudding in
    the mix
½ cup chocolate milk
⅓ cup butter or margarine, melted
3 eggs
1 container (16 oz) sour cream
1 package (4-serving size)
    chocolate fudge instant
    pudding and pie filling mix
1 bag (12 oz) semisweet chocolate
    chips (2 cups)

Rich Chocolate Glaze

¾ cup semisweet chocolate chips
3 tablespoons butter or margarine
3 tablespoons light corn syrup
1½ teaspoons water

1 Heat oven to 350°F. Generously grease 12-cup bundt cake pan with shortening; lightly flour.

2 In large bowl, mix cake mix, chocolate milk, butter, eggs, sour cream and pudding mix (dry) with spoon until well blended (batter will be very thick). Stir in chocolate chips. Spoon into pan.

3 Bake 55 to 65 minutes or until top springs back when touched lightly in center. Cool in pan 10 minutes. Turn pan upside down onto wire rack or heatproof serving plate; remove pan. Cool completely, about 2 hours.

4 In 1-quart saucepan, heat glaze ingredients over low heat, stirring frequently, until chocolate chips are melted and mixture is smooth. Drizzle glaze over cooled cake. Store loosely covered at room temperature.

1 Serving: Calories 460 (Calories from Fat 220); Total Fat 25g (Saturated Fat 13g); Cholesterol 75mg; Sodium 450mg; Total Carbohydrate 54g (Dietary Fiber 3g); Protein 5g

You don't want to lose even a drop of this divine batter, so measure the volume of your bundt cake pan using water to make sure it holds 12 cups. If the pan is smaller than 12 cups, the batter will overflow during baking.

Triple-Fudge Cake

Prep Time: 15 min ■ Start to Finish: 3 hrs 5 min ■ 15 Servings

⅓ cup sweetened condensed milk
1 cup semisweet chocolate chips (6 oz)
1 package chocolate fudge cake mix with pudding in the mix
½ cup vegetable oil
1 cup applesauce
2 eggs
½ cup chopped pecans

1 Heat oven to 350°F. Grease bottom only of 13×9-inch pan with shortening or spray bottom with cooking spray; coat with flour. In small microwavable bowl, microwave milk and ½ cup of the chocolate chips uncovered on Medium (50%) about 1 minute or until chocolate is softened; stir until smooth and set aside.

2 In large bowl, beat cake mix and oil with electric mixer on low speed 30 seconds (mixture will be crumbly); reserve 1 cup. Beat applesauce and eggs into remaining cake mixture on low speed 30 seconds (batter will be thick and grainy); beat on medium speed 2 minutes. Spread in pan.

3 Drop melted chocolate mixture by teaspoonfuls over batter, dropping more around edge than in center. Stir remaining ½ cup chocolate chips and the pecans into reserved cake mixture; sprinkle over batter. Bake 45 to 50 minutes or until center is set. Run knife around side of pan to loosen cake. Cool completely, about 2 hours.

1 Serving: Calories 330 (Calories from Fat 150); Total Fat 17g (Saturated Fat 5g); Cholesterol 30mg; Sodium 290mg; Total Carbohydrate 43g (Dietary Fiber 2g); Protein 4g

Cinnamon Streusel Coffee Cake

Prep Time: 10 min ■ Start to Finish: 35 min ■ 6 Servings

Streusel Topping
⅓ cup Original Bisquick® mix
⅓ cup packed brown sugar
½ teaspoon ground cinnamon
2 tablespoons firm butter or margarine

Coffee Cake
2 cups Original Bisquick mix
2/3 cup milk or water
2 tablespoons granulated sugar
1 egg

1 Heat oven to 375°F. Grease bottom and side of 9-inch round pan with shortening or cooking spray. In small bowl, mix ⅓ cup Bisquick mix, the brown sugar and cinnamon. With fork or pastry blender, cut in butter until mixture is crumbly; set aside.

2 In medium bowl, stir all coffee cake ingredients until blended. Spread in pan. Sprinkle with topping.

3 Bake 18 to 22 minutes or until golden brown. Serve warm or cool.

1 Serving: Calories 310 (Calories from Fat 110); Total Fat 12g (Saturated Fat 4.5g); Cholesterol 50mg; Sodium 720mg; Total Carbohydrate 46g (Dietary Fiber 0g); Protein 5g

Lemon–Poppy Seed Bundt Cake

Prep Time: 15 min ▪ Start to Finish: 3 hrs 10 min ▪ 16 Servings

Cake
1 package lemon cake mix with pudding in the mix
1¼ cups water
⅓ cup vegetable oil
3 eggs
2 tablespoons poppy seed

Lemon Glaze
1 cup powdered sugar
1 to 2 tablespoons lemon juice
¼ teaspoon grated lemon peel
 Grated lemon peel, if desired

1 Heat oven to 350°F. Grease 12-cup bundt cake pan with shortening; lightly flour.

2 In large bowl, beat cake mix, water, oil and eggs with electric mixer on low speed 30 seconds. Beat on medium speed 2 minutes, scraping bowl occasionally. Stir poppy seed into batter. Pour into pan.

3 Bake 38 to 43 minutes or until toothpick inserted in center comes out clean. Cool in pan 10 minutes. Turn pan upside down onto wire rack; remove pan. Cool completely, about 2 hours.

4 In a small bowl, stir powdered sugar, 1 tablespoon lemon juice and the lemon peel until blended. Stir in additional lemon juice, 1 teaspoon at a time, until smooth and consistency of thick syrup. Spread glaze over top of cake, allowing some to drizzle down side. Garnish with lemon peel. Store loosely covered at room temperature.

1 Serving: Calories 230 (Calories from Fat 80); Total Fat 9g (Saturated Fat 2g); Cholesterol 40mg; Sodium 240mg; Total Carbohydrate 34g (Dietary Fiber 0g); Protein 3g

Poppy seed can become rancid
if it is stored for a long period in your
cupboard. Stick it in your freezer, and it
will keep almost forever.

Caramel-Carrot Cake

Prep Time: 10 min ■ Start to Finish: 3 hrs ■ 15 Servings

1 package carrot cake mix with pudding in the mix
1 cup water
⅓ cup butter or margarine, melted
3 eggs
1 jar (16 to 17.5 oz) caramel or butterscotch topping
1 container (1 lb) vanilla ready-to-spread frosting

1 Heat oven to 350°F. Grease bottom only of 13×9-inch pan with shortening or spray bottom with cooking spray.

2 In large bowl, beat cake mix, water, butter and eggs in large bowl with electric mixer on low speed 30 seconds. Beat on medium speed 2 minutes. Pour into pan.

3 Bake 27 to 33 minutes or until toothpick inserted in center comes out clean. Cool 15 minutes. Poke top of warm cake every ½ inch with handle of wooden spoon, wiping handle occasionally to reduce sticking. Reserve ½ cup caramel topping. Drizzle remaining caramel topping evenly over top of cake; let stand about 15 minutes or until caramel topping has been absorbed into cake. Run knife around side of pan to loosen cake. Cover and refrigerate about 2 hours or until chilled.

4 Set aside 2 tablespoons of the reserved ½ cup caramel topping. Stir remaining topping into frosting; spread over top of cake. Drizzle with reserved 2 tablespoons caramel topping. Store covered in refrigerator.

1 Serving: Calories 450 (Calories from Fat 120); Total Fat 13g (Saturated Fat 7g); Cholesterol 55mg; Sodium 430mg; Total Carbohydrate 79g (Dietary Fiber 0g); Protein 3g

This gooey, rich cake needs to be joined by only a glass of milk or a cup of steaming coffee.

Margarita Cake

Prep Time: 20 min ■ Start to Finish: 3 hrs ■ 15 Servings

1½ cups coarsely crushed pretzels
½ cup sugar
½ cup butter or margarine, melted
1 package white cake mix with pudding in the mix
1¼ cups bottled nonalcoholic margarita mix
⅓ cup vegetable oil
1 tablespoon grated lime peel
3 egg whites
1 container (8 oz) frozen whipped topping, thawed
Grated lime peel, if desired

1 Heat oven to 350°F (325°F for dark or nonstick pans). Grease bottom only of rectangular pan, 13×9×2 inches, with shortening; lightly flour (or spray bottom with cooking spray; do not flour). In medium bowl, mix pretzels, sugar and butter. Sprinkle evenly on bottom of pan; press gently to form crust.

2 In large bowl, beat cake mix, margarita mix, oil, lime peel and egg whites in large bowl with electric mixer on low speed 30 seconds. Beat on medium speed 2 minutes, scraping bowl occasionally. Pour batter over pretzel mixture.

3 Bake 35 to 40 minutes or until light golden brown and top springs back when touched lightly in center. Cool completely, about 2 hours. Frost with whipped topping; sprinkle with lime peel. Store loosely covered in refrigerator.

Cut fat and calories in this cake by using fat-free whipped topping instead of regular whipped topping to frost the cake.

1 Serving: Calories 360 (Calories from Fat 140); Total Fat 16g (Saturated Fat 6g); Cholesterol 15mg; Sodium 400mg; Total Carbohydrate 52g (Dietary Fiber 0g); Protein 3g

Dulce de Leche Cake

Prep Time: 30 min ■ Start to Finish: 2 hrs 10 min ■ 12 Servings

½ cup butter (do not use margarine)
1 package butter-recipe yellow cake mix with pudding in the mix
1⅓ cups water
2 teaspoons vanilla
3 eggs
1 container (1 lb) caramel frosting

1 Heat oven to 350°F (325°F for dark or nonstick pans). Grease bottom only of 13×9-inch pan with shortening or spray with cooking spray.

2 In 1-quart saucepan, heat butter over medium heat 8 to 10 minutes, stirring frequently, just until golden brown. Remove from heat. Cool 15 minutes.

3 In large bowl, beat cake mix, browned butter, water, vanilla and eggs in large bowl with electric mixer on low speed 30 seconds. Beat on medium speed 2 minutes (brown flecks from butter will appear in batter). Pour into pan.

4 Bake 30 to 40 minutes or until cake is golden brown and toothpick inserted in center comes out clean. Cool completely, about 1 hour. Frost top of cake with frosting. Store loosely covered at room temperature.

You don't want to substitute margarine or vegetable oil spreads for the butter in this richly flavored recipe. Those products don't contain the milk proteins found in butter so they will not brown, but will burn instead.

1 Serving: Calories 440 (Calories from Fat 180); Total Fat 20g (Saturated Fat 11g); Cholesterol 75mg; Sodium 370mg; Total Carbohydrate 62g (Dietary Fiber 0g); Protein 4g

Luscious Mandarin Orange Cake

Prep Time: 10 min ■ Start to Finish: 1 hr 50 min ■ 15 Servings

Cake
1 package yellow cake mix with pudding in the mix
½ cup vegetable oil
½ cup chopped walnuts
4 eggs
1 can (11 oz) mandarin orange segments, undrained

Pineapple Frosting
1 can (20 oz) crushed pineapple, undrained
1 box (4-serving size) vanilla instant pudding and pie filling mix
1 cup frozen whipped topping, thawed

1 Heat oven to 350°F. Grease bottom only of 13×9-inch pan with shortening or cooking spray.

2 In large bowl, beat cake mix, oil, walnuts, eggs and orange segments (with juice) with electric mixer on low speed 30 seconds; beat on medium speed 2 minutes. Pour into pan.

3 Bake 35 to 40 minutes or until toothpick inserted in center comes out clean. Cool completely, about 1 hour.

4 In medium bowl, stir pineapple and pudding mix (dry) until mixed. Gently stir in whipped topping. Spread over cake. Store tightly covered in refrigerator.

For an extra-special touch, decorate this cake with curly strips of orange peel or sprinkle with toasted coconut to enhance the tropical flavors of the cake and frosting.

1 Serving: Calories 320 (Calories from Fat 130); Total Fat 15g (Saturated Fat 3.5g); Cholesterol 55mg; Sodium 340mg; Total Carbohydrate 44g (Dietary Fiber 1g); Protein 4g

Lemon-Raspberry Cake

Prep Time: 10 min ■ Start to Finish: 1 hr 40 min ■ 16 Servings

Cake
1 package lemon cake mix with pudding in the mix
1¼ cups water
⅓ cup vegetable oil
3 eggs
6 tablespoons raspberry preserves

Lemon Buttercream Frosting
1¼ cups butter or margarine, softened
2 teaspoons grated lemon peel
3 tablespoons lemon juice
3 cups powdered sugar

Garnish
Fresh raspberries, if desired

1 Heat oven to 350°F. Grease bottoms and sides of three 9-inch round pans with shortening or cooking spray; lightly flour. Make cake mix as directed on package, using water, oil and eggs. Pour into pans.

2 Bake 18 to 20 minutes or until toothpick inserted in center comes out clean. Cool 10 minutes; remove from pans to wire rack. Cool completely, about 1 hour.

3 In medium bowl, beat butter, lemon peel and lemon juice with electric mixer on medium speed 30 seconds. Gradually beat in powdered sugar. Beat 2 to 3 minutes longer or until light and fluffy.

4 On serving plate, place 1 cake layer, rounded side down. Spread with 3 tablespoons of the preserves. Add second layer, rounded side down. Spread with remaining 3 tablespoons preserves. Top with third layer, rounded side up. Frost side and top of cake with frosting. Store covered in refrigerator.

1 Serving: Calories 430 (Calories from Fat 200); Total Fat 22g (Saturated Fat 11g); Cholesterol 80mg; Sodium 330mg; Total Carbohydrate 54g (Dietary Fiber 0g); Protein 2g

Lemon Mousse Cake

Prep Time: 25 min ▪ Start to Finish: 2 hrs 10 min ▪ 12 to 16 Servings

1 package white cake mix with
    pudding in the mix
1¼ cups water
⅓ cup vegetable oil
3 egg whites

2 cups whipping cream
¼ cup powdered sugar
1 jar (10 oz) lemon curd
2 teaspoons grated lemon peel

1 Heat oven to 350°F. Grease bottoms only of two 8- or 9-inch round pans with shortening or spray with cooking spray.

2 In large bowl, beat cake mix, water, oil and egg whites in large bowl with electric mixer on low speed 30 seconds. Beat on medium speed 2 minutes, scraping bowl occasionally. Pour into pans.

3 Bake 8-inch rounds 27 to 32 minutes, 9-inch rounds 23 to 28 minutes, or until toothpick inserted in center comes out clean and center springs back when lightly touched in center. Cool 10 minutes. Run knife around side of pans to loosen cakes; remove from pans to wire rack. Cool completely, about 1 hour.

4 In chilled medium bowl, beat whipping cream and powdered sugar with electric mixer on high speed until stiff peaks form. Fold in lemon curd and lemon peel. Place 1 cake layer, rounded side down, on serving plate. Spread with 1 cup of the lemon mixture to within ¼ inch of edge. Top with second layer, rounded side up. Frost side and top of cake with remaining lemon mixture. Store loosely covered in refrigerator.

Lemon curd is a rich, tart custard made with sugar, lemon juice, lemon peel, butter and eggs. While you can make it from scratch, it's much easier to pick up a jar in the jams and jellies section of the supermarket.

1 Serving: Calories 440 (Calories from Fat 200); Total Fat 23g (Saturated Fat 10g); Cholesterol 45mg; Sodium 330mg; Total Carbohydrate 55g (Dietary Fiber 0g); Protein 4g

Almond-Orange Cake

Prep Time: 30 min ■ Start to Finish: 2 hrs 35 min ■ 12 Servings

Cake

1 cup slivered almonds

2 cups all-purpose flour

1 cup granulated sugar

⅓ cup slivered almonds, toasted*

1 cup fresh orange juice

½ cup butter or margarine, softened

1½ teaspoons almond extract

2 teaspoons baking powder

1 teaspoon salt

2 eggs

½ cup orange marmalade

Garnish

¾ cup whipping cream

2 tablespoons powdered or
    granulated sugar

Orange twist, if desired

1 Heat oven to 350°F (or 325°F if using dark or nonstick pan). Spray 9-inch springform pan with cooking spray. In food processor or blender, place 1 cup almonds; cover and process until almonds are finely ground. In large bowl, beat ground almonds and remaining cake ingredients except marmalade with electric mixer on low speed 30 seconds, scraping bowl constantly. Beat on high speed 3 minutes, scraping bowl occasionally. Pour batter into pan.

2 Bake 45 to 55 minutes or until top is evenly dark golden brown and cake springs back when touched lightly in center.

3 Cool in pan 10 minutes. Remove side of pan. Spread marmalade over top of cake. Cool completely, about 1 hour.

4 In chilled small bowl, beat whipping cream and 2 tablespoons sugar on high speed until soft peaks form. Spoon or pipe whipped cream around edge of cake; sprinkle ⅓ cup almonds over whipped cream. Refrigerate until serving. Garnish with orange twist.

*To toast nuts, bake uncovered in ungreased shallow pan at 350°F for 6 to 10 minutes, stirring occasionally, until golden brown.

1 Serving: Calories 390 (Calories from Fat 180); Total Fat 19g (Saturated Fat 9g); Cholesterol 70mg; Sodium 350mg; Total Carbohydrate 48g (Dietary Fiber 2g); Protein 6g

Watermelon Slices Cake

Prep Time: 30 min ▪ Start to Finish: 1 hr 45 min ▪ 16 Servings

1 package white cake mix with pudding in the mix
Water, oil and egg whites called for on cake mix package directions
1 package (0.13 oz) cherry or other red-colored unsweetened soft drink mix
½ cup plus 2 tablespoons miniature semisweet chocolate chips
1 container (12 oz) whipped fluffy white frosting
Green and red liquid food colors
⅔ cup green jelly beans

1 Heat oven to 350°F. Grease bottoms only of two 8- or 9-inch round pans with shortening or cooking spray. In large bowl, beat cake mix, water, oil, egg whites and drink mix with electric mixer on low speed 30 seconds; beat on medium speed 2 minutes, scraping bowl occasionally. Stir in ½ cup of the chocolate chips. Pour into pans.

2 Bake 8-inch rounds 27 to 32 minutes, 9-inch rounds 23 to 28 minutes, or until toothpick inserted in center comes out clean. Cool 10 minutes; remove from pans. Cool completely, about 1 hour.

3 In small bowl, stir 1 cup frosting with 10 to 20 drops green food color. Stir 10 to 20 drops red food color into remaining frosting. Frost sides of cakes with green frosting; press green jelly beans into frosting. Frost tops of cakes with red frosting; press remaining 2 tablespoons chocolate chips into frosting for seeds. To serve, cut into wedges.

1 Serving: Calories 350 (Calories from Fat 130); Total Fat 14g (Saturated Fat 4g); Cholesterol 0mg; Sodium 260mg; Total Carbohydrate 52g (Dietary Fiber 0g); Protein 2g

Caramel Cappuccino Cheesecake

Prep Time: 30 min ■ Start to Finish: 8 hrs 50 min ■ 16 Servings

Crust

1 ¼ cups chocolate cookie crumbs
   (from 15-oz box)

¼ cup butter or margarine, melted

Filling

2 tablespoons instant espresso
   coffee granules

2 teaspoons vanilla

4 packages (8 oz each) cream

cheese, softened

1½ cups granulated sugar

4 eggs

1 teaspoon ground cinnamon

¼ cup caramel topping (from a 16-oz jar)

Topping

1 cup whipping cream

2 tablespoons powdered sugar

¼ cup caramel topping (from a 16-oz jar)

1 Heat oven to 300°F. Wrap outside of 10-inch springform pan with foil. In small bowl, mix cookie crumbs and melted butter with fork. Press mixture evenly over bottom of pan. Refrigerate crust while preparing filling.

2 In small bowl, stir coffee granules and vanilla until coffee is dissolved; set aside.

3 In large bowl, beat cream cheese with electric mixer on medium speed until smooth. Gradually add 1½ cups sugar, beating until light and fluffy. Add eggs, one at a time, beating well after each addition. Add espresso mixture, cinnamon and ¼ cup caramel topping; beat about 30 seconds or until mixture is well blended. Pour over crust in pan.

4 Bake 1 hour 10 minutes to 1 hour 20 minutes or until cheesecake is set 1 ½ inches from edge and center is slightly jiggly. Turn oven off; open oven door at least 4 inches. Let cheesecake remain in oven 30 minutes. Remove cheesecake from oven. Run knife around edge of pan to loosen; cool 30 minutes at room temperature. Cover; refrigerate 6 hours or overnight.

5 Remove side of pan. In chilled medium bowl, beat 1 cup whipping cream and 2 tablespoons sugar on high speed until soft peaks form. Spread whipped cream over top of cheesecake; drizzle ¼ cup caramel topping over whipped cream.

1 Serving: Calories 440 (Calories from Fat 270); Total Fat 30g (Saturated Fat 18g); Cholesterol 140mg; Sodium 300mg; Total Carbohydrate 35g (Dietary Fiber 0g); Protein 7g

For a party-perfect cheesecake without cracks, try baking it in a water bath. Place filled foil-wrapped springform pan in a large roasting pan and pour enough boiling water into roasting pan to come halfway up sides of springform pan. Bake as directed.

Strawberry-Filled Cheesecake

Prep Time: 25 min ∎ Start to Finish: 7 hrs 10 min ∎ 12 Servings

1 cup graham cracker crumbs (about 16 squares)
¼ cup sugar
2 tablespoons butter or margarine, melted
3 packages (8 oz each) cream cheese, softened
1 cup sugar
4 eggs
1 teaspoon vanilla
1 container (8 oz) sour cream
1 can (21 oz) strawberry pie filling

1 Heat oven to 325°F. Wrap outside bottom and side of 10-inch springform pan with foil to prevent leaking. In small bowl, mix cracker crumbs and ¼ cup sugar; stir in butter. Press firmly and evenly in bottom of pan. Bake 12 to 15 minutes or until set.

2 In large bowl, beat cream cheese, 1 cup sugar, the eggs and vanilla with electric mixer on medium speed until smooth. Beat in sour cream. Spread half of mixture (about 3 cups) over crust. Spoon half of pie filling by tablespoonfuls onto cream cheese mixture. Top with remaining cream cheese mixture. (Refrigerate remaining pie filling.)

3 Bake 1 hour 5 minutes to 1 hour 15 minutes or until center is set. Cool 15 minutes. Run metal spatula carefully along side of cheesecake to loosen. Cool completely, about 1 hour. Cover and refrigerate at least 4 hours.

4 To serve, run metal spatula carefully along side of cheesecake to loosen again; remove foil and side of pan. Spoon remaining pie filling over cheesecake.

1 Serving: Calories 440 (Calories from Fat 250); Total Fat 28g (Saturated Fat 16g); Cholesterol 150mg; Sodium 250mg; Total Carbohydrate 40g (Dietary Fiber 0g); Protein 7g

Mango-Strawberry Sorbet Torte

Prep Time: 35 min ■ Start to Finish: 4 hrs 55 min ■ 16 Servings

Cake
1 package white cake mix with
    pudding in the mix
Water, vegetable oil and egg whites
    called for on cake mix package
1 pint (2 cups) mango sorbet, softened
1 pint (2 cups) strawberry sorbet,
    softened

Frosting
1½ cups whipping cream
½ cup powdered sugar
1 teaspoon grated lime peel
2 tablespoons lime juice

Garnish, if desired
Lime peel twists
Fresh strawberries

1 Heat oven to 350°F (325°F for dark or nonstick pan). Spray bottom only of 15×10×1-inch pan with baking spray with flour. Line with waxed paper; spray waxed paper.

2 In large bowl, make cake mix as directed on package, using water, oil and egg whites. Pour into pan. Bake 20 to 30 minutes or until toothpick inserted in center comes out clean. Cool in pan 10 minutes. Remove from pan to cooling rack; remove waxed paper. Cool completely, about 1 hour.

3 Cut cake crosswise into 3 equal sections. On long serving platter, place 1 section, rounded side down. Spread mango sorbet evenly over top. Place another cake section onto the sorbet; press gently onto sorbet. Spread with strawberry sorbet. Top with remaining cake section; press down gently. Cover lightly; freeze about 2 hours or until firm.

4 In large bowl, beat all frosting ingredients with electric mixer on high speed until stiff peaks form. Frost sides and top of torte. Freeze about 1 hour or until firm. Just before serving, garnish top with lime peel and strawberries. To serve, let stand at room temperature 10 minutes. Cut torte in half lengthwise, then cut crosswise into 8 slices for a total of 16 slices.

This is a great make-ahead dessert. Once it's frozen, cover tightly and freeze for up to 3 weeks.

1 Serving: Calories 330 (Calories from Fat 130); Total Fat 15g (Saturated Fat 6g); Cholesterol 25mg; Sodium 240mg; Total Carbohydrate 47g (Dietary Fiber 0g); Protein 3g

Double Chocolate–Cherry Torte

Prep Time: 30 min ■ Start to Finish: 6 hrs 35 min ■ 12 Servings

2 packages (8 oz each) semisweet
    baking chocolate, coarsely chopped
1 cup butter or margarine
6 eggs
1½ cups white chocolate chunks (from
    12-oz bag)

1½ cups whipping cream
4 oz cream cheese (from 8-oz package),
    softened
1 can (21 oz) cherry pie filling
¼ teaspoon almond extract
2 tablespoons amaretto liqueur,
    if desired

1 Heat oven to 400°F. Spray bottom and side of 9-inch springform pan with cooking spray. In 3-quart saucepan, melt semisweet chocolate and butter over medium-low heat, stirring constantly, until smooth. Cool 30 minutes.

2 In medium bowl, beat eggs with electric mixer on high speed about 5 minutes or until about triple in volume. Fold into chocolate mixture. Pour into springform pan. Bake 15 to 20 minutes or until edge is set but center is still soft and jiggles slightly when moved. Cool completely in pan, about 1½ hours. Then cover and refrigerate 1½ hours.

3 In medium microwavable bowl, mix white chocolate and 2 tablespoons whipping cream. Microwave uncovered on High 20 to 40 seconds, stirring once, until chocolate is melted. Stir until well blended. In medium bowl, beat cream cheese on medium speed until smooth. Gradually add white chocolate mixture, beating until smooth. Add 1 cup pie filling; beat until well blended and cherries are broken up.

4 In another chilled medium bowl, beat remaining whipping cream and almond extract on high speed until stiff peaks form. Fold in cherry-chocolate mixture until well blended. Spread over dark chocolate layer. Refrigerate at least 2 hours but no longer than 48 hours.

5 In medium bowl, stir remaining pie filling and liqueur until well blended. Remove side of springform pan. Serve torte topped with cherry sauce.

1 Serving: Calories 680 (Calories from Fat 440); Total Fat 49g (Saturated Fat 27g); Cholesterol 190mg; Sodium 190mg; Total Carbohydrate 51g (Dietary Fiber 3g); Protein 8g

You can use 1½ cups coarsely chopped white chocolate baking bars instead of the chunks.

Triple-Chocolate Torte

Prep Time: 15 min ■ Start to Finish: 6 hrs 35 min ■ 16 Servings

1 package (1 lb 3.8 oz) fudge brownie mix
¼ cup water
½ cup vegetable oil
2 eggs
1¼ cups milk
1 box (4-serving size) white chocolate instant pudding and pie filling mix
1 container (8 oz) frozen whipped topping, thawed
⅓ cup miniature semisweet chocolate chips
1 pint (2 cups) raspberries or strawberries, if desired

1 Heat oven to 325°F. Spray bottom only of 9-inch springform pan with cooking spray. Make brownie mix as directed on package, using water, oil and eggs. Spread in pan.

2 Bake 45 to 50 minutes or until toothpick inserted in center comes out clean. Cool completely, about 1 hour 30 minutes. (Do not remove side of pan.)

3 In large bowl, beat milk and pudding mix with wire whisk about 2 minutes or until thickened. Fold in whipped topping and chocolate chips. Pour over brownie.

4 Cover and freeze at least 4 hours before serving. Remove side of pan. Serve with raspberries. Store tightly covered in freezer.

1 Serving: Calories 300 (Calories from Fat 120); Total Fat 14g (Saturated Fat 5g); Cholesterol 30mg; Sodium 230mg; Total Carbohydrate 42g (Dietary Fiber 2g); Protein 3g

Strawberry–Cream Cheese Cupcakes

Prep Time: 20 min ■ Start to Finish: 1 hr 25 min ■ 24 Cupcakes

1 package yellow cake mix with pudding in the mix
1 container (8 oz) sour cream
½ cup vegetable oil
½ cup water
2 eggs
3 tablespoons strawberry preserves
1 package (3 oz) cream cheese, cut into 24 pieces
1 container (1 lb) cream cheese ready-to-spread frosting
Sliced fresh small strawberries, if desired

1 Heat oven to 350°F. Line 24 regular-size muffin cups with paper baking cups. In large bowl, mix cake mix, sour cream, oil, water and eggs in large bowl with spoon until well blended (batter will be thick). Divide batter evenly among muffin cups.

2 In small bowl; stir strawberry preserves until smooth. Place 1 piece of cream cheese on top of batter in each cupcake; press in slightly. Spoon ¼ measuring teaspoon of preserves over each cream cheese piece.

3 Bake 18 to 23 minutes or until tops are golden brown and spring back when touched lightly in center (some preserves may show in tops of cupcakes). Cool 10 minutes. Remove from pan to wire rack. Cool completely, about 30 minutes. Frost with frosting. Just before serving, garnish each cupcake with strawberry slices. Store covered in refrigerator.

You don't have to use strawberry; feel free to choose your favorite flavor of jam, jelly or preserves to tuck inside these fruity cake treats.

1 Cupcake: Calories 260 (Calories from Fat 120); Total Fat 13g (Saturated Fat 4.5g); Cholesterol 30mg; Sodium 200mg; Total Carbohydrate 32g (Dietary Fiber 0g); Protein 2g

Chocolate Chip Cheesecake Swirl Cupcakes

Prep Time: 30 min ■ Start to Finish: 1 hr 5 min ■ 24 Cupcakes

½ cup sugar	¼ cup unsweetened baking cocoa
2 packages (3 oz each) cream cheese, softened	2 teaspoons baking soda
	1 teaspoon salt
1 egg	1¼ cups water
1 cup semisweet chocolate chips (6 oz)	½ cup vegetable oil
2¼ cups all-purpose flour	2 tablespoons white vinegar
1⅔ cups sugar	2 teaspoons vanilla

1 Heat oven to 350°F. Line 24 regular-size muffin cups with paper baking cups. In medium bowl, beat ½ cup sugar and the cream cheese with electric mixer on medium speed until smooth. Beat in egg. Stir in chocolate chips; set aside.

2 In large bowl, beat all remaining ingredients on low speed 30 seconds, scraping bowl occasionally. Beat on high speed 3 minutes, scraping bowl occasionally. Reserve 1½ cups batter.

3 Fill each muffin cup with about 1 rounded tablespoonful batter (⅓ full). Spoon 1 tablespoon cream cheese mixture onto batter in each cup. Top each with about ½ rounded tablespoon reserved batter.

4 Bake 30 to 35 minutes or until toothpick inserted in center comes out clean.

These cream cheese-swirl cupcakes are great for picnics. They can be made the day before, so they'll be ready to serve to kids of all ages!

1 Cupcake: Calories 220 (Calories from Fat 90); Total Fat 10g (Saturated Fat 3.5g); Cholesterol 15mg; Sodium 230mg; Total Carbohydrate 32g (Dietary Fiber 1g); Protein 2g

Key West Cupcakes

Prep Time: 25 min ■ Start to Finish: 1 hr 30 min ■ 24 Cupcakes

Filling

1 box (4-serving size) vanilla instant
    pudding and pie mix
1½ cups whipping cream
¼ cup fresh Key lime juice
4 drops green food coloring
1½ cups powdered sugar

Cupcakes

1 box yellow cake mix with pudding in
    the mix
Water, vegetable oil and eggs called
    for on mix box

Frosting

1 container (12 oz) whipped fluffy
    white frosting
1 tablespoon fresh Key lime juice
½ teaspoon grated Key lime peel

1 In large bowl, beat pudding mix and whipping cream with wire whisk 2 minutes. Let stand 3 minutes. Beat in ¼ cup lime juice and the food color; stir in powdered sugar until smooth. Cover; refrigerate.

2 Heat oven to 350°F. Place paper baking cup in each of 24 regular-size muffin cups. Make and bake cake mix as directed on box for 24 cupcakes, using water, oil and eggs. Cool in pan 10 minutes; remove from pan to cooling rack. Cool completely, about 30 minutes.

3 Spread 1 rounded tablespoonful filling on top of each cupcake. Stir frosting in container 20 times. Gently stir in 1 tablespoon lime juice and the lime peel. Spoon frosting into 1-quart resealable food-storage plastic bag. Cut ½-inch opening from the bottom former of bag. Squeeze 1 tablespoon frosting from bag onto filling on each cupcake. Store covered in refrigerator.

Key limes are smaller than regular limes. If you can't find then, purchase a bottle of Key lime juice, or use regular limes.

1 Cupcake: Calories 280 (Calories from fat 120); Total Fat 13g (Saturated Fat 5g); Cholesterol 45mg; Sodium 230mg; Total Carbohydrate 38g (Dietary Fiber 0g); Protein 2g

Molten Chocolate Cupcakes

Prep Time: 30 min ∎ Start to Finish: 2 hrs ∎ 18 Cupcakes

½ cup whipping cream
1 cup semisweet chocolate chips (6 oz)
1 package devil's food cake mix with pudding in the mix
1 cup water
⅓ cup vegetable oil
3 eggs
1 container (1 lb) chocolate frosting
Powdered sugar, if desired
Sliced strawberries, if desired

1 In 1-quart saucepan, heat whipping cream over medium-high heat until hot but not boiling. Stir in chocolate chips until melted and mixture is smooth. Refrigerate about 1 hour, stirring occasionally, until thick.

2 Heat oven to 350°F (325°F for dark or nonstick pans). Spray 18 large muffin cups with baking spray with flour. In large bowl, beat cake mix, water, oil and eggs with electric mixer on low speed 30 seconds; beat on medium speed 2 minutes, scraping bowl constantly. Place ¼ cup batter in each muffin cup. Spoon 1 tablespoon cold chocolate mixture on top of batter in center of each cup.

3 Bake 18 to 22 minutes or until top springs back when lightly touched. Cool 1 minute. Carefully remove from pan; place on cooking parchment paper. Cool 10 minutes. Frost with chocolate frosting. Just before serving, dust with powdered sugar; garnish with strawberry slices. Serve warm.

1 Cupcake: Calories 340 (Calories from Fat 150); Total Fat 17g (Saturated Fat 6g); Cholesterol 45mg; Sodium 320mg; Total Carbohydrate 43g (Dietary Fiber 1g); Protein 3g

Chocolate Cupcakes
with White Truffle Frosting

Prep Time: 35 min ■ Start to Finish: 1 hr 10 min ■ 24 Cupcakes

1 package devil's food cake mix with pudding in the mix
Water, vegetable oil and eggs called for on cake mix package directions
1 cup white vanilla baking chips
1 container (1 lb) vanilla frosting

1 Heat oven to 350°F (325°F for dark or nonstick pans). Place paper baking cup in each of 24 regular-size muffin cups. Make and bake cake mix as directed on package for 24 cupcakes, using water, oil and eggs. Cool in pan 10 minutes; remove from pan to cooling rack. Cool completely, about 30 minutes.

2 In medium microwavable bowl, microwave baking chips uncovered on Medium (50%) 4 to 5 minutes, stirring after 2 minutes. Stir until smooth; cool 5 minutes. Stir into frosting until well blended. Immediately frost cupcakes or pipe frosting on cupcakes.

3 If desired, tie ribbons around cupcakes for decoration. Store loosely covered.

You can decorate these basic cupcakes any way you like. Use colored sugar, edible glitter or any purchased decoration.

1 Cupcake: Calories 270 (Calories from Fat 120); Total Fat 13g (Saturated Fat 5g); Cholesterol 25mg; Sodium 240mg; Total Carbohydrate 36g (Dietary Fiber 0g); Protein 2g

Frosted Cupcake Cones

Prep Time: 20 min ∎ Start to Finish: 2 hrs 35 min ∎ 30 to 36 Cupcake Cones

1 package cake mix (any non-swirl flavor) with pudding in the mix
Water, oil and eggs called for on cake mix package
30 to 36 flat-bottom ice cream cones
1 tub (12 oz) whipped frosting (any flavor)
Assorted candies, cookies, miniature chocolate chips or colored candy
sprinkles, if desired

1 Heat oven to 350°F. Make cake mix as directed on package, using water, oil and eggs. Fill each cone about half full of batter. Stand cones in muffin pan.

2 Bake 20 to 25 minutes or until toothpick carefully inserted in center comes out clean. Cool completely, about 1 hour. Frost with frosting; decorate with candies. Store loosely covered at room temperature.

Fill cones halfway so the cake won't rise too high and flow over the edges.

1 Cupcake Cone: Calories 150 (Calories from Fat 50); Total Fat 6g (Saturated Fat 2.5g); Cholesterol 20mg; Sodium 120mg; Total Carbohydrate 24g (Dietary Fiber 0g); Protein 1g

Sour Cream–Pear Fold-Over Pie

No-Bake Lime Chiffon Pie

Fluffy Strawberry Pie

Macadamia Nut–Banana Cream Pie

Orange Swirl Pumpkin Pie

Chocolate Pecan Pie

Chocolate Truffle Pie

Fudgy Brownie Pie with Caramel Sauce

Decadent Chocolate Tart

Banana–Chocolate Mousse Tart

Fabulous Three-Berry Tart

Blueberry-Almond Tart

Orange–Cream Cheese Tart

Piña Colada Tart

Pear Tartlets

Nectarine-Plum Crostata

Dutch Apple Wedges

4

pies
and
tarts

Sour Cream–Pear Fold-Over Pie

Prep Time: 30 min ■ Start to Finish: 1 hr 30 min ■ 8 Servings

Filling
²⁄₃ cup sugar
½ cup sour cream
½ cup golden or dark raisins
¼ cup all-purpose flour
1 teaspoon ground cinnamon
4 cups ½-inch slices peeled pears
(about 3 medium)

Pastry
1 cup all-purpose flour
½ teaspoon salt
⅓ cup plus 1 tablespoon shortening
2 to 3 tablespoons cold water

Topping
¼ cup coarsely chopped walnuts
1 to 2 tablespoons milk, if desired
1 tablespoon sugar, if desired

1 Heat oven to 425°F. In large bowl, stir all filling ingredients except pears until mixed. Fold in pears; set aside.

2 In medium bowl, mix 1 cup flour and the salt. With fork or pastry blender, cut in shortening until particles are size of small peas. Sprinkle with cold water, 1 tablespoon at a time, tossing with fork until all flour is moistened and pastry almost cleans side of bowl (1 to 2 teaspoons more water can be added if necessary).

3 Gather pastry into a ball. Shape into flattened round on lightly floured surface. Roll pastry into 13-inch circle. Place on ungreased large cookie sheet.

4 Mound filling on center of pastry to within 3 inches of edge. Sprinkle walnuts over filling. Fold edge of pastry over filling, overlapping to make about 12 pleats and leaving 6-inch circle of filling showing in center. Brush milk over pastry; sprinkle with 1 tablespoon sugar.

5 Bake 30 to 35 minutes, covering crust with foil for the last 10 to 15 minutes to prevent burning if necessary, until crust is golden brown and filling is bubbly in center. Cool 30 minutes. Cut into wedges. Serve warm.

1 Serving: Calories 370 (Calories from Fat 140); Total Fat 16g (Saturated Fat 4.5g); Cholesterol 10mg; Sodium 150mg; Total Carbohydrate 52g (Dietary Fiber 4g); Protein 4g

No-Bake Lime Chiffon Pie

Prep Time: 20 min ■ Start to Finish: 2 hrs 20 min ■ 8 Servings

⅓ cup lime juice
1 envelope unflavored gelatin (2 teaspoons)
1 teaspoon grated lime peel
½ cup fat-free sweetened condensed milk (from 14-oz can)
2 drops green food color, if desired
1 drop yellow food color, if desired
4 cups frozen fat-free whipped topping, thawed (from 12-oz container)
1 graham cracker crumb crust (6 oz)
2 thin lime slices, cut into quarters, if desired

1 In 1-quart saucepan, place lime juice; sprinkle with gelatin. Let stand 1 minute to soften. Heat over medium heat about 2 minutes, stirring occasionally, until gelatin is dissolved. Remove from heat; cool slightly. Stir in lime peel.

2 In medium bowl, mix condensed milk and food colors. Stir in lime juice mixture. Using rubber spatula, fold in all but ¼ cup of the whipped topping. Spread in pie crust, smoothing top. Cover; refrigerate at least 2 hours or until firm.

3 Before serving, garnish pie with remaining ¼ cup whipped topping and lime slices.

To keep this pie picture-perfect, use the plastic cover that came with the crust as a protective cover; just turn it upside down over the pie.

1 Serving: Calories 230 (Calories from Fat 70); Total Fat 8g (Saturated Fat 2.5g); Cholesterol 0mg; Sodium 105mg; Total Carbohydrate 37g (Dietary Fiber 0g); Protein 3g

Fluffy Strawberry Pie

Prep Time: 30 min ▪ Start to Finish: 9 hrs 30 min ▪ 8 Servings

Pretzel Crust
1¼ cups crushed pretzels
¼ cup granulated sugar
½ cup butter or margarine, melted

Filling
1 box (4-serving size) strawberry-flavored gelatin
¾ cup boiling water
1 teaspoon grated lime peel
¼ cup lime juice
1½ cups whipping cream
¾ cup powdered sugar
2 cups strawberries, slightly crushed
Chocolate-covered strawberries, if desired

1 In medium bowl, mix all crust ingredients. Press mixture firmly and evenly against bottom and side of ungreased 9-inch glass pie plate.

2 In large bowl, place gelatin. Pour boiling water over; stir until gelatin is dissolved. Stir in lime peel and lime juice. Refrigerate about 1 hour or until very thick but not set.

3 Beat gelatin mixture with electric mixer on high speed about 4 minutes or until thick and fluffy; set aside. In chilled large bowl, beat whipping cream and powdered sugar on high speed until stiff peaks form. Fold whipped cream and crushed strawberries into gelatin mixture. Pour into crust.

4 Refrigerate about 8 hours or until set. Garnish with chocolate-covered strawberries. Store loosely covered in refrigerator.

1 Serving: Calories 420 (Calories from Fat 260); Total Fat 29g (Saturated Fat 16g); Cholesterol 90mg; Sodium 310mg; Total Carbohydrate 39g (Dietary Fiber 1g); Protein 3g

Macadamia Nut–Banana Cream Pie

Prep Time: 40 min ■ Start to Finish: 3 hrs 15 min ■ 8 Servings

Crust

1¼ cups all purpose flour

½ cup macadamia nuts, finely chopped

⅓ cup butter or margarine, softened

2 tablespoons granulated sugar

½ teaspoon vanilla

1 egg, beaten

Filling

⅔ cup granulated sugar

¼ cup cornstarch

½ teaspoon salt

3 cups whole milk

4 egg yolks

2 tablespoons butter or margarine

1 tablespoon vanilla

2 large bananas, sliced

Topping

1 cup whipping cream

2 tablespoons powdered or granulated sugar

½ cup macadamia nuts, coarsely chopped, toasted

1 In medium bowl, beat all crust ingredients with electric mixer on low speed about 1 minute or just until blended. Press mixture evenly in bottom and up side of ungreased 9-inch glass pie plate; prick mixture with fork. Refrigerate 30 minutes while preparing filling.

2 In 2-quart saucepan, mix ⅔ cup sugar, the cornstarch and salt. In large bowl, beat milk and egg yolks with wire whisk until blended; gradually stir into sugar mixture. Cook over medium-low heat about 15 minutes, stirring constantly, until mixture thickens and boils. Boil 2 minutes, beating constantly with wire whisk; remove from heat. Beat in 2 tablespoons butter and 1 tablespoon vanilla with wire whisk. Press plastic wrap on filling to prevent a skin from forming. Cool at room temperature while baking crust.

3 Heat oven to 400°F. Bake crust 16 to 18 minutes or until edge is golden brown. Cool at room temperature 15 minutes. Place banana slices on pie crust. Stir filling well; pour filling over bananas. Press plastic wrap on filling; refrigerate at least 2 hours until thoroughly chilled.

4 In chilled small bowl, beat whipping cream and 2 tablespoons sugar on high speed until soft peaks form; spread over top of pie. Sprinkle with toasted nuts.

1 Serving: Calories 590 (Calories from Fat 330); Total Fat 36g (Saturated Fat 17g); Cholesterol 200mg; Sodium 320mg; Total Carbohydrate 55g (Dietary Fiber 3g); Protein 9g

To toast nuts, bake uncovered in ungreased shallow pan in 350°F oven 6 to 10 minutes, stirring occasionally, until golden brown.

Orange Swirl Pumpkin Pie

Prep Time: 25 min ■ Start to Finish: 3 hrs 15 min ■ 8 Servings

1 refrigerated pie crust (from 15-oz box), softened as directed on box

1 can (14 oz) sweetened condensed milk

2 eggs

1 package (3 oz) cream cheese, softened

¼ cup orange marmalade

1 can (15 oz) pumpkin (not pumpkin pie mix)

1 teaspoon pumpkin pie spice

1 cup whipping cream

2 tablespoons orange marmalade

Orange peel curls, if desired

1 Heat oven to 350°F. Place pie crust in 9-inch glass pie plate as directed on box for one-crust filled pie.

2 In large bowl, beat milk and eggs with electric mixer on medium speed until smooth. In medium bowl, beat cream cheese and ¼ cup marmalade on medium speed until well blended. Add 2 tablespoons milk-egg mixture to cream cheese mixture; beat on medium speed until smooth.

3 Add pumpkin and pie spice to remaining milk-egg mixture; beat on medium speed until smooth. Carefully pour into crust-lined pie plate. Drop cream cheese mixture by spoonfuls over pumpkin mixture. With a butter knife, carefully swirl cream cheese mixture into pumpkin mixture. Cover edge of crust with 2- to 3-inch strip of foil to prevent excessive browning; remove foil during last 15 minutes of baking. Bake 50 to 55 minutes or until set and knife inserted in center comes out clean. Cool completely, about 2 hours.

4 In chilled medium bowl, beat whipping cream and 2 tablespoons marmalade on high speed until soft peaks form. Top pie or individual servings with whipped cream and orange peel curls.

Beat the whipping cream up to 2 hours ahead of time and store in the refrigerator until serving

1 Serving: Calories 490 (Calories from Fat 230); Total Fat 26g (Saturated Fat 14g); Cholesterol 120mg; Sodium 240mg; Total Carbohydrate 56g (Dietary Fiber 2g); Protein 8g

Chocolate Pecan Pie

Prep Time: 20 min ■ Start to Finish: 4 hrs 25 min ■ 8 Servings

One-Crust Flaky Pastry
1 cup all-purpose flour
½ teaspoon salt
⅓ cup plus 1 tablespoon shortening
2 to 3 tablespoons cold water

Chocolate Pecan Filling
⅔ cup sugar
⅓ cup butter or margarine, melted

1 cup corn syrup
2 tablespoons bourbon, if desired
½ teaspoon salt
3 eggs
1 cup pecan halves or broken pecans
1 bag (6 oz) semisweet chocolate chips (1 cup)

1 Heat oven to 375°F. In medium bowl, mix flour and ½ teaspoon salt. With fork or pastry blender, cut in shortening until particles are size of small peas. Sprinkle with cold water, 1 tablespoon at a time, tossing with fork until all flour is moistened and pastry almost cleans side of bowl (1 to 2 teaspoons more water can be added if necessary).

2 Gather pastry into a ball. Shape into flattened round on lightly floured surface. Wrap flattened round of pastry in plastic wrap and refrigerate about 45 minutes or until dough is firm and cold, yet pliable. This allows the shortening to become slightly firm, which helps make the baked pastry more flaky. If refrigerated longer, let pastry soften slightly before rolling.

3 Roll pastry on lightly floured surface, using floured rolling pin, into circle 2 inches larger than upside-down 9-inch glass pie plate. Fold pastry into fourths; place in pie plate. Unfold and ease into plate, pressing firmly against bottom and side. Trim overhanging edge of pastry 1 inch from rim of pie plate. Fold and roll pastry under, even with edge of plate; flute as desired.

4 In large bowl, beat sugar, butter, corn syrup, bourbon, salt and eggs with hand beater. Stir in pecans and chocolate chips. Pour into pastry-lined pie plate. Cover edge of crust with 2- to 3-inch strip of foil to prevent excessive browning; remove foil during last 15 minutes of baking.

5 Bake 40 to 50 minutes or until set. Cool 30 minutes. Refrigerate about 2 hours or until chilled.

1 Serving: Calories 640 (Calories from Fat 320); Total Fat 35g (Saturated Fat 12g); Cholesterol 100mg; Sodium 420mg; Total Carbohydrate 75g (Dietary Fiber 3g); Protein 6g

Chocolate Truffle Pie

Prep Time: 25 min ▪ Start to Finish: 3 hrs ▪ 12 Servings

Crust
1¼ cups chocolate cookie crumbs
¼ cup butter or margarine, melted

Filling
1 bag (12 oz) semisweet chocolate
    chips (2 cups)
1 cup whipping cream
1 teaspoon vanilla
2 egg yolks

Topping
½ cup whipping cream
1 tablespoon powdered sugar
Unsweetened baking cocoa, if
    desired

1 In small bowl, mix cookie crumbs and butter. In ungreased 9-inch pie plate, press crumb mixture in bottom and 1 inch up.

2 In double boiler set over hot simmering water, heat chocolate chips 2 to 3 minutes, stirring frequently, until melted and smooth. Gradually add 1 cup whipping cream, stirring constantly, until combined. Stir in vanilla and egg yolks until well blended. Cook over medium-low heat 5 to 6 minutes, stirring frequently, until thickened and hot. Pour filling into crust. Refrigerate at least 3 hours or until firm.

3 In medium bowl, beat ½ cup whipping cream and the powdered sugar with electric mixer on high speed 1 to 2 minutes or until soft peaks form. Top individual servings with whipped cream. Dust with cocoa.

Don't own a double boiler? Place a small saucepan in a larger skillet or saucepan filled with 1 to 2 inches of simmering water.

1 Serving: Calories 350 (Calories from Fat 220); Total Fat 24g (Saturated Fat 14g); Cholesterol 80mg; Sodium 125mg; Total Carbohydrate 30g (Dietary Fiber 2g); Protein 3g

Fudgy Brownie Pie
with Caramel Sauce

Prep Time: 15 min ■ Start to Finish: 2 hrs 5 min ■ 16 Servings

Crust
1 refrigerated pie crust (from
    15-oz box), softened as
    directed on box

Filling
1 cup butter or margarine
2 cups sugar
2 teaspoons vanilla
4 eggs, slightly beaten

1½ cups all-purpose flour
¾ cup unsweetened baking cocoa
¼ teaspoon salt
1 cup semisweet chocolate chunks
    (from 11.5- or 12-oz bag)
1 cup chopped pecans

Sauce
1 bag (14 oz) caramels, unwrapped
⅔ cup half-and-half

1 Heat oven to 350°F. Place pie crust in 9-inch glass pie plate as directed on box for one-crust filled pie.

2 In 2-quart saucepan, melt butter over low heat; remove from heat. Stir in sugar, vanilla and eggs until well blended. Stir in flour, cocoa and salt until smooth. Stir in chocolate chunks and pecans. Spread evenly in pie crust.

3 Bake 45 to 50 minutes or until set. Cool 1 hour.

4 Meanwhile, in 2-quart saucepan, heat caramels and half-and-half over low heat, stirring constantly, until caramels are melted and mixture is smooth. Drizzle hot caramel sauce over each serving.

1 Serving: Calories 560 (Calories from Fat 250); Total Fat 28g (Saturated Fat 13g); Cholesterol 90mg; Sodium 260mg; Total Carbohydrate 70g (Dietary Fiber 3g); Protein 6g

Decadent Chocolate Tart

Prep Time: 40 min ▪ Start to Finish: 2 hrs 50 min ▪ 12 Servings

Crust

⅓ cup butter or margarine, softened

¼ cup powdered sugar

½ cup all-purpose flour

2 tablespoons unsweetened baking cocoa

Filling

¼ cup butter or margarine

4 oz semisweet baking chocolate

¼ cup granulated sugar

2 eggs

¼ cup sour cream

2 tablespoons all-purpose flour

Topping

2 oz semisweet baking chocolate

1 tablespoon butter or margarine

1 tablespoon honey

2 kiwifruit, cut up

1 can (11 oz) mandarin orange segments, drained

1 Heat oven to 350°F. Grease 9-inch tart pan with removable bottom with shortening. In medium bowl, beat ⅓ cup butter and the powdered sugar with electric mixer on medium speed until blended. Beat in ½ cup flour and the cocoa until coarse crumbs form. Press mixture evenly in bottom of tart pan.

2 Bake 5 to 7 minutes or until set. Meanwhile, in 1-quart saucepan, heat ¼ cup butter and 4 ounces chocolate over low heat 2 to 3 minutes, stirring constantly, until melted and smooth. Set aside to cool.

3 In large bowl, beat granulated sugar and eggs with mixer on high speed 3 to 4 minutes, scraping bowl frequently, until foamy and light in color. Add sour cream, 2 tablespoons flour and the chocolate mixture; beat 1 to 2 minutes, scraping bowl frequently, until blended. Spread filling over crust.

4 Bake 20 to 25 minutes or until firm to the touch. Cool 15 minutes. Remove side of pan. Cool completely, about 30 minutes.

5 In 1-quart saucepan, heat 2 ounces chocolate, 1 tablespoon butter and the honey over low heat 2 to 3 minutes, stirring constantly, until melted and smooth. Spread chocolate mixture over tart. Lightly press fruit around outer edge of tart. Refrigerate until firm, about 1 hour. Let stand at room temperature about 20 minutes before serving.

1 Serving: Calories 260 (Calories from Fat 150); Total Fat 16g (Saturated Fat 10g); Cholesterol 65mg; Sodium 85mg; Total Carbohydrate 26g (Dietary Fiber 2g); Protein 3g

Banana–Chocolate Mousse Tart

Prep Time: 20 min ■ Start to Finish: 3 hrs 10 min ■ 10 Servings

Pastry	Filling
1⅓ cups all-purpose flour	1 package (4-serving size) chocolate
½ teaspoon salt	pudding and pie filling mix (not instant)
½ cup shortening	1½ cups milk
3 to 4 tablespoons cold water	2 oz semisweet baking chocolate, chopped
	1½ cups frozen (thawed) whipped topping
	3 bananas, sliced

1 Heat oven to 400°F. In medium bowl, mix flour and salt. With fork or pastry blender, cut in shortening until particles are size of small peas. Sprinkle with cold water, 1 tablespoon at a time, tossing with fork until all flour is moistened and pastry almost cleans side of bowl (1 to 2 teaspoons more water can be added if necessary).

2 On lightly floured surface, roll pastry into 13-inch circle, about ⅛ inch thick. Press mixture evenly in bottom and up side of ungreased 10-inch tart pan with removable bottom. Trim pastry even with top of pan. Prick bottom and side of pastry with fork.

3 Bake 15 to 20 minutes or until golden brown. Cool completely, about 30 minutes.

4 Meanwhile, in 2-quart saucepan, heat pudding mix and milk over medium heat, stirring occasionally, until mixture boils. Stir in chopped chocolate until melted. Pour into medium bowl; place plastic wrap directly on surface of pudding mixture. Refrigerate about 1 hour or until completely cooled.

5 Fold ½ cup of the whipped topping into cooled chocolate mixture. Arrange banana slices in single layer in bottom of baked crust. Spoon chocolate mixture over bananas. Refrigerate about 1 hour or until thoroughly chilled. Garnish with remaining 1 cup whipped topping and additional banana slices, if desired.

1 Serving: Calories 310 (Calories from Fat 140); Total Fat 16g (Saturated Fat 6g); Cholesterol 0mg; Sodium 190mg; Total Carbohydrate 38g (Dietary Fiber 2g); Protein 4g

Fabulous Three-Berry Tart

Prep Time: 30 min ■ Start to Finish: 2 hrs 30 min ■ 10 Servings

Crust
1 bag (8 oz) animal crackers
⅓ cup butter or margarine, melted
1 teaspoon ground cinnamon
2 tablespoons sugar

Filling
1 package (8 oz) cream cheese, softened
½ cup sugar
2 tablespoons lemon juice
1 cup whipping cream
½ pint (1 cup) fresh blackberries
½ pint (1 cup) fresh raspberries
½ pint (1 cup) fresh blueberries
¼ cup strawberry jam
1 tablespoon orange juice

1 Heat oven to 350°F. Place animal crackers in food processor; cover and process about 1 minute or until finely ground. In medium bowl, mix cracker crumbs, butter, cinnamon and 2 tablespoons sugar. Press mixture evenly in bottom and up side of ungreased 9-inch tart pan with removable bottom. Bake 8 to 12 minutes or until golden brown. Cool completely, about 20 minutes.

2 In large bowl, beat cream cheese, ½ cup sugar and the lemon juice with electric mixer on low speed until blended. Add whipping cream; beat on high speed 3 to 5 minutes or until light and fluffy. Spread mixture in tart shell. Refrigerate at least 2 hours.

3 Arrange berries on chilled filling. In small microwavable bowl, microwave jam uncovered on High about 20 seconds or until warm. Stir in orange juice; mix well with fork. Brush strawberry glaze over berries.

1 Serving: Calories 410 (Calories from Fat 220); Total Fat 25g (Saturated Fat 14g); Cholesterol 70mg; Sodium 220mg; Total Carbohydrate 41g (Dietary Fiber 3g); Protein 4g

Blueberry-Almond Tart

Prep Time: 15 min ∎ Start to Finish: 1 hr ∎ 6 Servings

2 cups blueberries
⅓ cup sugar
1½ tablespoons cornstarch
2 tablespoons water
¼ teaspoon almond extract
1 refrigerated pie crust (from 15-oz box), softened as directed on box
½ cup sliced almonds
1 teaspoon decorator sugar crystals

1 Heat oven to 400°F. Grease cookie sheet with shortening or spray with cooking spray. In large bowl, mix blueberries, sugar, cornstarch, water and almond extract.

2 Remove pie crust from pouch; unroll on cookie sheet. Spread ¼ cup of the almonds over crust; lightly press into crust.

3 Spoon blueberry mixture onto center of crust to within 2 inches of edge of crust. Fold 2-inch edge of crust over blueberry mixture, crimping crust slightly and leaving a circle of blueberry mixture showing. Sprinkle crust edge with sugar crystals.

4 Bake 20 minutes. Sprinkle remaining ¼ cup almonds over blueberry mixture. Bake 5 to 10 minutes longer or until crust is golden. Cool 15 minutes.

1 Serving: Calories 290 (Calories from Fat 120); Total Fat 13g (Saturated Fat 3.5g); Cholesterol 0mg; Sodium 150mg; Total Carbohydrate 40g (Dietary Fiber 2g); Protein 2g

Orange–Cream Cheese Tart

Prep Time: 30 min ▪ Start to Finish: 3 hrs 10 min ▪ 10 Servings

Pastry

1 cup all-purpose flour

½ teaspoon salt

⅓ cup plus 1 tablespoon shortening

2 to 3 tablespoons cold water

Filling

1 package (8 oz) cream cheese, softened

1½ cups milk

1 package (4-serving size) vanilla instant
    pudding and pie filling mix

1 can (15 oz) mandarin orange segments,
    well drained and patted dry

¾ cup orange marmalade

½ oz semisweet baking chocolate, grated

1 Heat oven to 450°F. In medium bowl, mix flour and salt. With fork or pastry blender, cut in shortening until particles are size of small peas. Sprinkle with cold water, 1 tablespoon at a time, tossing with fork until all flour is moistened and pastry almost cleans side of bowl (1 to 2 teaspoons more water can be added if necessary).

2 On lightly floured surface, roll pastry into 13-inch circle, about ⅛ inch thick. Press pastry in bottom and up side of ungreased 10-inch tart pan with removable bottom. Trim pastry even with top of pan. Prick bottom and side of pastry with fork.

3 Bake 9 to 11 minutes or until light golden brown. Cool completely, about 30 minutes.

4 In small bowl, beat cream cheese with electric mixer on medium speed until creamy. Gradually beat in milk. Beat in pudding mix. Spoon into tart crust; spread evenly. Top with orange segments.

5 In small microwavable bowl, microwave marmalade uncovered on High 20 to 30 seconds or until warm. Brush or spoon marmalade over orange segments. Refrigerate about 2 hours or until firm. Garnish with grated chocolate.

1 Serving: Calories 340 (Calories from Fat 160); Total Fat 17g (Saturated Fat 8g); Cholesterol 30mg; Sodium 360mg; Total Carbohydrate 43g (Dietary Fiber 1g); Protein 5g

Piña Colada Tart

Prep Time: 15 min ■ Start to Finish: 1 hr 45 min ■ 12 Servings

1 refrigerated pie crust (from 15-oz box), softened as directed on box
¼ cup sugar
¼ cup cornstarch
1 cup canned cream of coconut (not coconut milk)
1 cup whole milk
2 egg yolks
1 tablespoon butter or margarine

2 tablespoons dark rum or 1½ teaspoons rum extract
1 can (20 oz) sliced pineapple, drained, slices cut in half
¼ cup apricot jam
1 tablespoon dark rum or orange juice
2 tablespoons coconut, toasted*

1 Heat oven to 425°F. Place pie crust in ungreased 10-inch tart pan with removable bottom. Press pie crust in bottom and up side of pan. Trim crust even with top of pan. Prick bottom and side of crust with fork. Bake 9 to 11 minutes or until lightly browned. Cool on wire rack.

2 Meanwhile, in 2-quart saucepan, mix sugar and cornstarch. In small bowl, mix cream of coconut, milk and egg yolks; gradually stir into sugar mixture. Cook over medium heat, stirring constantly, until mixture thickens and boils. Boil and stir 1 minute; remove from heat. Beat in butter and 2 tablespoons rum with wire whisk. Cool at room temperature 1 hour.

3 Pour cooled pie filling into baked tart shell. Arrange pineapple slices in decorative pattern over filling. In small microwavable bowl, microwave jam uncovered on High 20 seconds. Stir in 1 tablespoon rum; mix well with fork. Brush glaze over pineapple. Sprinkle with toasted coconut. Refrigerate until serving.

*To toast coconut, bake uncovered in ungreased shallow pan in 350°F oven 5 to 7 minutes, stirring occasionally, until golden brown.

1 Serving: Calories 250 (Calories from Fat 130); Total Fat 14g (Saturated Fat 9g); Cholesterol 40mg; Sodium 95mg; Total Carbohydrate 29g (Dietary Fiber 1g); Protein 2g

Cream of coconut is a canned mixture of coconut paste, water and sugar. It is available in supermarkets and in liquor stores.

Pear Tartlets

Prep Time: 10 min ▪ Start to Finish: 40 min ▪ 4 Tartlets

1 sheet frozen puff pastry (from 17.3-oz package), thawed as directed on
    package
1 ripe pear
¼ cup peach preserves

1 Heat oven to 400°F. Cut pastry into 4 squares. Place pastry squares on
ungreased cookie sheet.

2 Peel pear and cut into quarters; remove seeds. Slice each pear quarter into
very thin slices. Arrange pear slices over pastry squares, leaving ½-inch
border.

3 Bake about 20 minutes or until pastry is puffed and browned. Spread 1
tablespoon preserves over top of each warm tartlet to cover pears. Cool
on cookie sheet 10 minutes before serving.

This is the perfect dessert to make when you're short on time.
Keep puff pastry in the freezer for those occasions when you need a quick
dessert.

1 Tartlet: Calories 420 (Calories from Fat 210); Total Fat 24g (Saturated Fat 8g); Cholesterol 75mg;
Sodium 160mg; Total Carbohydrate 48g (Dietary Fiber 2g); Protein 5g

Nectarine-Plum Crostata

Prep Time: 20 min ∎ Start to Finish: 1 hr 30 min ∎ 8 Servings

Pastry

1 ½ cups all-purpose flour
1 teaspoon sugar
¼ teaspoon salt
½ cup firm butter or margarine,
 cut into pieces
1 egg yolk
4 to 5 tablespoons cold water

Filling

½ cup sugar
3 tablespoons all-purpose flour
¼ teaspoon ground cinnamon
3 cups sliced nectarines (about 3 medium)
2 cups sliced plums (about 2 medium)
1 tablespoon lemon juice
2 tablespoons butter or margarine, softened
1 tablespoon sugar, if desired

1 Heat oven to 425°F. In medium bowl, mix 1½ cups flour, 1 teaspoon sugar and the salt. With fork or pastry blender, cut in ½ cup butter, until mixture is crumbly. Stir in egg yolk with fork. Sprinkle with water, 1 tablespoon at a time, tossing with fork until ball forms. Gather pastry into a ball; flatten to ½-inch thickness. Wrap in plastic wrap and refrigerate 30 minutes.

2 On lightly floured surface, roll pastry into 13-inch circle, about ⅛ inch thick. Place on ungreased large cookie sheet. In large bowl, mix ½ cup sugar, 3 tablespoons flour and the cinnamon. Stir in nectarines and plums until coated. Sprinkle with lemon juice; mix. Spoon fruit mixture onto center of pastry, spreading to within 3 inches of edge. Dot with 2 tablespoons butter. Fold edge of pastry over fruit mixture, making pleats and leaving circle of fruit mixture showing. Brush edge of pastry with water; sprinkle with 1 tablespoon sugar.

3 Bake 30 to 40 minutes, covering foil for last 10 to 15 minutes, if necessary, to prevent overbrowning, until crust is dark golden brown and fruit is tender. Cool completely, about 1 hour.

You can keep a fruit crostata at room temperature for 2 days; after that, store it loosely covered in the fridge up to 2 days longer. In warm or humid climates, always store in the fridge.

1 Serving: Calories 340 (Calories from Fat 140); Total Fat 16g (Saturated Fat 8g); Cholesterol 65mg; Sodium 170mg; Total Carbohydrate 45g (Dietary Fiber 3g); Protein 4g

Dutch Apple Wedges

Prep Time: 25 min ■ Start to Finish: 1 hr 35 min ■ 12 Servings

Crust
1 cup all-purpose flour
⅓ cup sugar
½ cup butter or margarine

Crumb Topping
⅔ cup all-purpose flour
½ cup packed brown sugar
¼ cup butter or margarine

Apple Topping
⅓ cup sugar
2 tablespoons all-purpose flour
¾ teaspoon ground cinnamon
1½ cups thinly sliced peeled tart cooking apples

1 Heat oven to 350°F. In medium bowl, mix 1 cup flour and ⅓ cup sugar. With fork or pastry blender, cut in ½ cup butter until crumbly. Press mixture evenly in bottom of ungreased 9-inch round pan. Bake 25 minutes.

2 Meanwhile, in a small bowl, mix all Crumb Topping ingredients until crumbly; set aside.

3 In medium bowl, mix ⅓ cup sugar, 2 tablespoons flour and the cinnamon. Stir in apples until coated. Spoon apple mixture over baked crust. Sprinkle with Crumb Topping.

4 Bake about 30 minutes or until topping is light brown and apples are tender. Cool 30 minutes before serving. Serve warm or cool. Cut into 12 wedges.

1 Serving: Calories 260 (Calories from Fat 110); Total Fat 12g (Saturated Fat 6g); Cholesterol 30mg; Sodium 80mg; Total Carbohydrate 36g (Dietary Fiber 0g); Protein 2g

Tart cooking apples perfect for this dessert include Granny Smith, Greening and Haralson.

Ice Cream with Marinated Strawberries

Summer Fruit–Topped Sorbet Sundae

Orange Sorbet and Raspberry Parfaits

Ginger-Peach Dessert

Ultimate Frozen Mud Pie Dessert

Frozen Angel Toffee Dessert

S'mores Chocolate Chip Ice Cream Sandwiches

Frosty Pumpkin Squares

Frozen Cinnamon-Chocolate Dessert

Chocolate-Banana Frozen Squares

Blueberry-Topped Lemon Ice Cream Pie

Cherry-Chocolate Ice Cream Pie

"Jamocha" Ice Cream Pie

Mint-Chocolate Ice Cream Cake

Chocolate Malt Ice Cream Cake

Mud Slide Ice Cream Cake

Brownie Ice Cream Cake

Banana Split Cake

Frozen Strawberry Cheesecake

White Chocolate–Cherry Chip Ice Cream Cake

5

frozen
desserts

Ice Cream with Marinated Strawberries

Prep Time: 15 min ■ Start to Finish: 2 hrs 15 min ■ 8 Servings

1 quart (4 cups) fresh strawberries
½ cup powdered sugar
¼ cup orange-flavored liqueur or orange juice
1 quart (4 cups) strawberry or vanilla ice cream

1 Cut strawberries in half; place in large bowl. Sprinkle with powdered sugar and liqueur; stir gently. Cover and refrigerate about 2 hours.

2 Spoon strawberries over ice cream.

1 Serving: Calories 210 (Calories from Fat 70); Total Fat 8g (Saturated Fat 5g); Cholesterol 30mg; Sodium 60mg; Total Carbohydrate 32g (Dietary Fiber 2g); Protein 3g

Summer Fruit–Topped Sorbet Sundae

Prep Time: 10 min ■ Start to Finish: 40 min ■ 4 Servings

1 large nectarine, chopped (1 cup)
¾ cup fresh raspberries
¾ cup fresh blueberries
2 tablespoons sugar
2 teaspoons orange-flavored liqueur or orange juice
1 pint (2 cups) lemon sorbet
4 thin ginger cookies

1 In small bowl, mix nectarine, raspberries, blueberries, sugar and liqueur. Refrigerate at least 30 minutes but no longer than 4 hours.

2 Into each of 4 serving dishes, scoop ½ cup sorbet. Stir fruit mixture; spoon over sorbet. Garnish each serving with 1 cookie.

Let guests build their own desserts! Set up a sundae bar with ice cream toppings and syrups and extras such as fresh strawberries, sliced bananas, chopped nuts and candies.

1 Serving: Calories 250 (Calories from Fat 10); Total Fat 1g (Saturated Fat 0g); Cholesterol 0mg; Sodium 50mg; Total Carbohydrate 57g (Dietary Fiber 3g); Protein 1g

Orange Sorbet and Raspberry Parfaits

Prep Time: 15 min ▪ Start to Finish: 15 min ▪ 4 Servings

1 pint (2 cups) fresh raspberries
2 tablespoons sugar
2 tablespoons orange or raspberry liqueur
4 slices (about ¾ inch thick) frozen pound cake (from 10.75-oz package),
    thawed
1 pint (2 cups) orange sorbet

1 Reserve about ¼ cup of the raspberries for garnish. In medium bowl, mix remaining raspberries, the sugar and liqueur.

2 Cut pound cake into ¾-inch cubes. Layer half of the cake, half of the sorbet and half of the raspberry mixture in each of 4 parfait glasses. Repeat layers. Sprinkle with reserved raspberries. Serve immediately.

If you don't have parfait glasses, layer this dessert in champagne or wine goblets or fancy dessert dishes. Add a touch of color with a sprig of fresh mint.

1 Serving: Calories 520 (Calories from Fat 170); Total Fat 19g (Saturated Fat 8g); Cholesterol 80mg; Sodium 80mg; Total Carbohydrate 83g (Dietary Fiber 5g); Protein 5g

Ginger-Peach Dessert

Prep Time: 15 min ■ Start to Finish: 5 hrs 30 min ■ 12 Servings

Gingersnap Crust
40 gingersnap cookies (about 1½ inches in diameter)
½ cup pecan pieces
½ cup butter or margarine, melted

Ginger-Peach Filling
2 quarts (8 cups) peach frozen yogurt, softened
1 container (8 oz) frozen reduced-fat whipped topping, thawed
¼ cup finely chopped pecans
2 medium peaches, cut into thin slices

1 Heat oven to 350°F. Make Gingersnap Crust by placing cookies and pecans in food processor. Cover and process until crushed. Add butter; process until mixed. Press evenly in ungreased rectangular pan, 13×9×2 inches. Bake 8 to 10 minutes or until center is set when lightly touched. Cool completely, about 25 minutes. Spread frozen yogurt over cooled crust. Freeze 30 minutes.

2 Spread whipped topping over frozen yogurt; sprinkle with pecans. Freeze about 4 hours or until firm.

3 To serve, let stand at room temperature 5 to 10 minutes. Cut dessert into squares. Top each square with 2 or 3 peach slices.

1 Serving: Calories 470 (Calories from Fat 180); Total Fat 20g (Saturated Fat 9g); Cholesterol 30mg; Sodium 290mg; Total Carbohydrate 64g (Dietary Fiber 2g); Protein 9g

The frozen yogurt needs to be just soft enough so you can scoop and spread it; soften it by placing in the fridge for 20 to 30 minutes. If you let it stand at room temperature, it will become too soft on the outside but remain too firm on the inside.

Ultimate Frozen Mud Pie Dessert

Prep Time: 15 min ■ Start to Finish: 1 hr 25 min ■ 9 Servings

1 pint (2 cups) coffee-flavored frozen yogurt
¾ cup chocolate cookie crumbs
2 tablespoons sugar
2 tablespoons butter or margarine, melted
½ cup caramel topping
2 tablespoons finely chopped pecans
1¼ cups frozen (thawed) fat-free whipped topping

1 Remove frozen yogurt from freezer to soften. Spray 8-inch square pan with cooking spray. In small bowl, mix cookie crumbs and sugar. Stir in butter until crumbly and well blended. Press mixture evenly in bottom of pan. Freeze about 10 minutes or until set.

2 Spread slightly softened yogurt evenly over crust. Freeze about 1 hour or until firm.

3 In small bowl, mix caramel topping and pecans. To serve, top each serving with generous 2 tablespoons whipped topping. Carefully pour 1 tablespoon caramel mixture over top.

Chocolate cookie crumbs can be purchased in a 15-ounce box in the baking aisle of your grocery store.

1 Serving: Calories 220 (Calories from Fat 60); Total Fat 6g (Saturated Fat 3g); Cholesterol 10mg; Sodium 180mg; Total Carbohydrate 38g (Dietary Fiber 0g); Protein 3g

Frozen Angel Toffee Dessert

Prep Time: 20 min ▪ Start to Finish: 4 hrs 40 min ▪ 15 Servings

1 package white angel food cake mix
1¼ cups cold water
6 bars (1.4 oz each) chocolate-covered English toffee candy
1 container (8 oz) frozen whipped topping, thawed
Cocoa powder, if desired

1 Move oven rack to lowest position (remove other racks). Heat oven to 350°F.

2 In extra-large glass or metal bowl, beat cake mix and water with electric mixer on low speed 30 seconds; beat on medium speed 1 minute. Pour into ungreased 10-inch angel food (tube) cake pan. (Do not use fluted tube cake pan or 9-inch angel food pan or batter will overflow.)

3 Bake 37 to 47 minutes or until top is dark golden brown and cracks feel very dry and not sticky. Do not underbake. Immediately turn pan upside down onto glass bottle until cake is completely cool, about 2 hours. Run knife around edges of cake; remove from pan.

4 Crush or finely chop candy bars; reserve ⅓ cup. Fold remaining crushed candy into whipped topping.

5 Tear cake into about 1-inch pieces. In large bowl, mix cake pieces and whipped topping mixture. Lightly press cake mixture in ungreased 13×9-inch pan. Sprinkle with reserved crushed candy. Freeze dessert about 1 hour 30 minutes or until firm. Cut into squares or spoon into dessert dishes. Dust with cocoa powder. Store covered in freezer.

1 Serving: Calories 240 (Calories from Fat 70); Total Fat 8g (Saturated Fat 5g); Cholesterol 10mg; Sodium 310mg; Total Carbohydrate 39g (Dietary Fiber 0g); Protein 3g

S'Mores Chocolate Chip Ice Cream Sandwiches

Prep Time: 15 min ■ Start to Finish: 3 hrs 15 min ■ 8 Sandwiches

About 3 tablespoons marshmallow creme
16 fudge-covered graham cookies (1½×1 ¾ inches each)
½ cup chocolate chip ice cream

1 Spoon about 1 teaspoon marshmallow creme on the flat side of 1 cookie. Top with about ½ tablespoon ice cream. Top with another cookie, flat side down, pressing gently. Place in shallow pan; immediately place in freezer. Repeat for remaining sandwiches, placing each in freezer as made.

2 Freeze at least 3 hours until firm. Wrap individually in plastic wrap or waxed paper.

These frozen treats make a fun summer dessert. To serve a crowd, make a double or triple batch.

1 Sandwich: Calories 100 (Calories from Fat 40); Total Fat 4.5g (Saturated Fat 3.5g); Cholesterol 0mg; Sodium 50mg; Total Carbohydrate 13g (Dietary Fiber 0g); Protein 0g

Frosty Pumpkin Squares

Prep Time: 15 min ■ Start to Finish: 4 hrs 45 min ■ 9 Servings

1 quart (4 cups) vanilla ice cream
1¼ cups graham cracker crumbs (about 20 squares)
¼ cup butter or margarine, melted
1 cup canned pumpkin (not pumpkin pie mix)
½ cup packed brown sugar
½ teaspoon salt
½ teaspoon ground cinnamon
½ teaspoon ground ginger
¼ teaspoon ground nutmeg

1 Let ice cream stand at room temperature 30 to 45 minutes to soften.

2 Meanwhile, in small bowl, mix cracker crumbs and butter; reserve 2 to 3 tablespoons crumb mixture. In ungreased 8- or 9-inch square pan, press remaining crumb mixture firmly and evenly over bottom.

3 In large bowl, beat remaining ingredients with wire whisk until well blended. Stir in ice cream with spoon. Spread over crumb mixture in pan. Sprinkle reserved crumb mixture over top.

4 Freeze uncovered at least 4 hours or until top of pumpkin mixture is firm, then cover and return to freezer. Let stand at room temperature 15 to 20 minutes before cutting.

This is a great make-ahead recipe. Prepare and freeze up to 2 weeks before. For easy cutting, let stand at room temperature for 15 to 20 minutes.

1 Serving: Calories 290 (Calories from Fat 120); Total Fat 13g (Saturated Fat 7g); Cholesterol 40mg; Sodium 290mg; Total Carbohydrate 38g (Dietary Fiber 1g); Protein 3g

Frozen Cinnamon-Chocolate Dessert

Prep Time: 15 min ▪ Start to Finish: 2 hrs 40 min ▪ 8 Servings

Dessert
1 cup chocolate water cookie crumbs (about 20 cookies)
¼ cup butter or margarine, melted
1 quart (4 cups) cinnamon, vanilla or chocolate ice cream, slightly softened

Cinnamon-Chocolate Sauce
½ cup whipping cream
¼ cup sugar
1 oz unsweetened baking chocolate, chopped
½ teaspoon ground cinnamon

1 In small bowl, mix cookie crumbs and butter. Press mixture evenly in bottom of ungreased 8-inch springform pan. Freeze 10 minutes.

2 Spoon ice cream onto crumb crust; smooth top. Cover and freeze about 2 hours or until firm.

3 In 1-quart saucepan, heat whipping cream, sugar and chocolate to boiling over medium heat, stirring constantly. Boil and stir about 30 seconds or until chocolate is melted; remove from heat. Stir in cinnamon. Continue stirring 3 to 4 minutes or until thoroughly mixed, glossy and slightly thickened.

4 Remove dessert from freezer 15 minutes before serving. Run metal spatula along side of dessert to loosen; remove side of pan. Serve dessert with warm or cool sauce. Store dessert loosely covered in freezer.

For a sweet alternative to the chocolate sauce, heat 1 cup caramel topping with ½ teaspoon ground cinnamon until warm.

1 Serving: Calories 360 (Calories from Fat 200); Total Fat 22g (Saturated Fat 13g); Cholesterol 65mg; Sodium 190mg; Total Carbohydrate 35g (Dietary Fiber 2g); Protein 4g

Chocolate-Banana Frozen Squares

Prep Time: 15 min ■ Start to Finish: 4 hrs 15 min ■ 9 Servings

1 cup graham cracker crumbs (about 16 squares)
3 tablespoons fat-free caramel topping
1 quart fat-free chocolate ice cream or frozen yogurt, softened
¼ cup fat-free caramel topping
2 bananas, sliced
½ cup frozen fat-free whipped topping, thawed
2 tablespoons graham cracker crumbs
Maraschino cherries, if desired

1 Spray 8-inch square glass baking dish with cooking spray. In medium bowl, mix 1 cup cracker crumbs and 3 tablespoons caramel topping. Press evenly in bottom of pan.

2 Spoon half of the softened ice cream onto crust, spreading evenly. Drizzle with ¼ cup caramel topping. Spoon remaining ice cream over topping, spreading evenly. Cover and freeze about 4 hours or until firm.

3 For serving pieces, cut dessert into 3 rows by 3 rows. Place squares on serving plates. Top with banana slices, whipped topping, 2 tablespoons cracker cracker crumbs and cherries.

In this recipe, fat-free caramel topping replaces the traditional butter or margarine to hold the graham cracker crust together.

1 Serving: Calories 200 (Calories from Fat 10); Total Fat 1g (Saturated Fat 0g); Cholesterol 0mg; Sodium 170mg; Total Carbohydrate 43g (Dietary Fiber 1g); Protein 3g

Blueberry-Topped Lemon Ice Cream Pie

Prep Time: 10 min ■ Start to Finish: 5 hrs 35 min ■ 8 Servings

1 package (6 oz) ready-to-use vanilla wafer cookie crust
1 pint (2 cups) vanilla ice cream, slightly softened
1 pint (2 cups) lemon sherbet, slightly softened
½ cup fresh or frozen blueberries (no need to thaw)
¼ cup blueberry preserves
1 tablespoon lemon juice
Grated lemon peel, if desired

1 Heat oven to 375°F. Bake cookie crust 5 minutes. Cool completely, about 20 minutes. Spread 1 cup of the vanilla ice cream over bottom of cooled crust. Freeze 30 minutes.

2 Spread lemon sherbet over ice cream. Freeze 30 minutes.

3 Spread remaining ice cream over sherbet. Freeze at least 4 hours until firm.

4 In small bowl, mix blueberries, preserves and lemon juice; refrigerate until serving. Serve 1 tablespoon blueberry mixture over each slice of pie. Garnish with lemon peel.

Switch up the flavor by using orange sherbet for the pie, orange juice for the topping and grated orange peel for the garnish.

1 Serving: Calories 350 (Calories from Fat 140); Total Fat 16g (Saturated Fat 6g); Cholesterol 20mg; Sodium 250mg; Total Carbohydrate 48g (Dietary Fiber 3g); Protein 4g

Cherry-Chocolate Ice Cream Pie

Prep Time: 30 min ■ Start to Finish: 2 hrs 40 min ■ 8 Servings

15 creme-filled chocolate sandwich cookies, crumbled
¼ cup butter or margarine, melted
¾ cup hot fudge topping (room temperature)
1 quart (4 cups) vanilla ice cream, softened
¼ cup sugar
1 tablespoon cornstarch
½ cup water
2 tablespoons frozen cranberry juice cocktail concentrate
2 cups fresh or frozen dark sweet cherries, halved, pitted
1 tablespoon cherry-flavored liqueur, if desired

1 Heat oven to 375°F. In food processor, place crumbled cookies. Cover; process 10 to 15 seconds or until finely crushed. Add melted butter. Cover; process 5 to 10 seconds or until mixed. Press mixture evenly in bottom and up side of ungreased 9-inch pie plate. Bake 8 to 10 minutes or until set. Cool completely, about 30 minutes.

2 Stir hot fudge topping until smooth. Carefully spread over bottom of crust. Freeze 30 minutes. Spread ice cream over hot fudge topping. Cover; freeze at least 1 hour until firm.

3 Meanwhile, in 2-quart saucepan, mix sugar, cornstarch, water and frozen juice concentrate. Heat to boiling over medium heat, stirring occasionally. Stir in cherries; reduce heat. Simmer 5 minutes. Stir in liqueur. Cool completely, about 30 minutes. Let pie stand 10 minutes before cutting. Serve sauce over slices of frozen pie.

1 Serving: Calories 460 (Calories from Fat 180); Total Fat 20g (Saturated Fat 11g); Cholesterol 50mg; Sodium 320mg; Total Carbohydrate 63g (Dietary Fiber 3g); Protein 5g

"Jamocha" Ice Cream Pie

Prep Time: 20 min ■ Start to Finish: 4 hrs 20 min ■ 8 Servings

Coffee Pat-in-Pan Pie Crust
1 cup all-purpose flour
½ cup butter or margarine, softened
2 teaspoons instant coffee granules or crystals

Ice Cream Filling
1 quart (4 cups) coffee ice cream, slightly softened
¾ cup hot fudge topping
1 cup frozen (thawed) whipped topping, if desired
Coffee-flavored chocolate candies or chocolate-covered coffee beans, if desired

1 Heat oven to 400°F. In medium bowl, mix crust ingredients with spoon until dough forms. Press dough firmly and evenly against bottom and side of ungreased 9-inch pie plate. Bake 12 to 15 minutes or until light brown. Cool completely, about 45 minutes.

2 Spread 1 pint of the ice cream in pie crust. Cover and freeze about 1 hour or until firm.

3 Spread hot fudge topping over ice cream in pie crust. Carefully spread remaining pint of ice cream over topping. Cover and freeze at least 2 hours until firm but no longer than 2 weeks.

4 To serve, let stand at room temperature about 10 minutes before cutting. Garnish with whipped topping and candies just before serving.

1 Serving: Calories 410 (Calories from Fat 200); Total Fat 22g (Saturated Fat 12g); Cholesterol 65mg; Sodium 230mg; Total Carbohydrate 47g (Dietary Fiber 2g); Protein 6g

Mint-Chocolate Ice Cream Cake

Prep Time: 25 min ∎ Start to Finish: 5 hrs 50 min ∎ 16 Servings

Cake

1 package butter recipe chocolate cake mix with pudding in the mix

Water, butter and eggs called for on mix package

Filling

1½ quarts (6 cups) green mint-flavored ice cream with chocolate chips or chocolate swirl, slightly softened

Frosting

1½ cups whipping cream

2 tablespoons powdered sugar

4 drops green food color

1 Heat oven to 350°F (325°F for dark or nonstick pans). Grease bottoms only of two 9-inch round cake pans; line bottoms with waxed paper. Make cake mix as directed on package, using water, butter and eggs. Spoon evenly into pans.

2 Bake as directed on package for 9-inch pans or until toothpick inserted in center comes out clean. Cool in pans 10 minutes. Remove from pans to cooling racks. Remove waxed paper. Cool completely, about 30 minutes.

3 Line 9-inch round cake pan with foil. Spoon and spread ice cream evenly in pan. Cover with foil; freeze until completely frozen, about 2 hours.

4 On serving plate, place 1 cake layer with rounded side down. Remove ice cream from pan; peel off foil. Place on top of cake. Top with remaining cake layer, rounded side up.

5 In medium bowl, beat whipping cream, powdered sugar and food color on high speed until stiff peaks form. Frost side and top of cake with whipped cream. Freeze about 2 hours or until firm. Let stand at room temperature 10 minutes before serving.

This dessert, wrapped with foil, will keep up to a month in the freezer. You can also make the ice cream layer ahead of time and freeze it.

1 Serving: Calories 380 (Calories from Fat 200); Total Fat 22g (Saturated Fat 13g); Cholesterol 105mg; Sodium 360mg; Total Carbohydrate 41g (Dietary Fiber 1g); Protein 5g

Chocolate Malt Ice Cream Cake

Prep Time: 30 min ■ Start to Finish: 7 hrs 5 min ■ 16 Servings

1½ cups all-purpose flour
1 cup sugar
¼ cup unsweetened baking cocoa
1 teaspoon baking soda
½ teaspoon salt
⅓ cup vegetable oil
1 teaspoon white vinegar
1 teaspoon vanilla
1 cup water

1 cup chocolate fudge topping
1½ quarts (6 cups) vanilla ice cream,
   slightly softened
2 cups malted milk ball candies,
   coarsely chopped
1 cup whipping cream
¼ cup chocolate fudge topping
Additional whole malted milk ball
   candies, if desired

1 Heat oven to 350°F. Grease bottom and side of 9- or 10-inch springform pan with shortening; lightly flour. In large bowl, mix flour, sugar, cocoa, baking soda and salt with spoon. Add oil, vinegar, vanilla and water; stir vigorously about 1 minute or until well blended. Immediately pour into pan.

2 Bake 30 to 35 minutes or until toothpick inserted in center comes out clean. Cool completely, about 1 hour.

3 Spread 1 cup fudge topping over cake. Freeze about 1 hour or until topping is firm.

4 In 3-quart bowl, mix ice cream and coarsely chopped candies; spread over cake. Freeze about 4 hours or until ice cream is firm.

5 In chilled medium bowl, beat whipping cream with electric mixer on high speed until stiff peaks form. Remove side of pan; place cake on serving plate. Top with whipped cream.

6 In small microwavable bowl, microwave fudge topping uncovered on High 30 seconds or until thin enough to drizzle. Drizzle over whipped cream. Garnish with additional whole candies.

1 Serving: Calories 430 (Calories from Fat 180); Total Fat 20g (Saturated Fat 10g); Cholesterol 40mg; Sodium 310mg; Total Carbohydrate 58g (Dietary Fiber 2g); Protein 5g

Mud Slide Ice Cream Cake

Prep Time: 30 min ■ Start to Finish: 6 hrs ■ 15 Servings

> 1 package chocolate fudge cake mix with pudding in the mix
> ½ cup butter or margarine, melted
> 2 eggs
> 2 tablespoons coffee-flavored liqueur or strong coffee
> 1 quart (4 cups) vanilla ice cream
> 1 container (12 oz) whipped chocolate frosting
> 2 tablespoons coffee-flavored liqueur, if desired

1 Heat oven to 350°F (325°F for dark or nonstick pan). Grease bottom only of 13×9-inch pan with shortening or cooking spray.

2 In large bowl, mix cake mix, butter and eggs with spoon. Spread in pan. Bake 20 to 25 minutes or until center is set (top will appear dry and cracked). Cool completely, about 1 hour.

3 Brush 2 tablespoons liqueur over cake. Let ice cream stand about 15 minutes at room temperature to soften. Spread ice cream over cake. Freeze 3 hours or until firm.

4 In medium bowl, mix frosting and 2 tablespoons liqueur; spread over ice cream. Freeze at least 1 hour.

Coffee lovers can substitute coffee-flavored ice cream for the vanilla.

1 Serving: Calories 380 (Calories from Fat 160); Total Fat 18g (Saturated Fat 8g); Cholesterol 60mg; Sodium 400mg; Total Carbohydrate 51g (Dietary Fiber 2g); Protein 4g

Brownie Ice Cream Cake

Prep Time: 25 min ▪ Start to Finish: 3 hrs 55 min ▪ 16 Servings

1 package (1 lb 6.5 oz) supreme brownie mix (with chocolate syrup pouch)
Water, vegetable oil and eggs called for on brownie mix package directions
½ gallon (8 cups) vanilla ice cream, slightly softened
1 cup hot fudge topping, warmed if desired
2 tablespoons candy sprinkles
16 red maraschino cherries with stems, drained

1 Heat oven to 350°F. Line two 9-inch round cake pans with foil; grease bottoms only with shortening or cooking spray.

2 Make brownie mix as directed on package, except divide batter evenly between pans. Bake 22 to 26 minutes or until toothpick inserted 2 inches from side of pan comes out almost clean. Cool completely in pans, about 1 hour. Do not remove from pans.

3 Spread slightly softened ice cream evenly on brownies in pans. Freeze at least 2 hours or until ice cream is firm.

4 Remove cakes from pans; remove foil. Place on serving plates. Cut each cake into 8 wedges. Drizzle each wedge with hot fudge topping. Decorate with candy sprinkles and cherries. Store covered in freezer.

1 Serving: Calories 370 (Calories from Fat 140); Total Fat 15g (Saturated Fat 6g); Cholesterol 60mg; Sodium 200mg; Total Carbohydrate 54g (Dietary Fiber 2g); Protein 5g

Banana Split Cake

Prep Time: 25 min ■ Start to Finish: 2 hrs 15 min ■ 12 Servings

Cake

1 package yellow cake mix
1 box (4-serving size) banana instant
    pudding and pie filling mix
¾ cup vegetable oil
¾ cup buttermilk
1 teaspoon vanilla
4 eggs
2 ripe bananas, mashed (about ¾ cup)

Toppings

1½ quarts (6 cups) vanilla ice cream
1 box (10 oz) frozen sweetened sliced
    strawberries, thawed
¾ cup hot fudge sauce
¾ cup frozen whipped topping,
    thawed
12 maraschino cherries with stems

1 Heat oven to 350°F (325°F for dark or nonstick pan). Spray bottom only of 13×9-inch pan with baking spray with flour. In large bowl, beat all cake ingredients with electric mixer on low speed 30 seconds. Beat on medium speed 2 minutes. Pour into pan.

2 Bake 50 to 55 minutes or until deep golden brown and toothpick inserted in center comes out clean. Cool completely, about 1 hour. Cut cake in half lengthwise, then cut crosswise into 12 slices for a total of 24 slices.

3 Place 2 cake slices in each banana split dish or parfait glass. Top each serving with 2 small scoops of ice cream. Spoon strawberries over one scoop. Drizzle hot fudge sauce over other scoop. Top each with whipped topping and cherry.

If you don't have long banana split or parfait dishes, you can cut the cake into squares and use round dessert bowls.

1 Serving: Calories 640 (Calories from Fat 270); Total Fat 30g (Saturated Fat 11g); Cholesterol 105mg; Sodium 560mg; Total Carbohydrate 85g (Dietary Fiber 2g); Protein 7g

Frozen Strawberry Cheesecake

Prep Time: 25 min ■ Start to Finish: 6 hrs 15 min ■ 10 Servings

Crust

2 tablespoons butter or margarine, melted

¼ cup old-fashioned oats

¼ cup finely chopped walnuts

3 tablespoons ground flaxseed or flaxseed meal

2 tablespoons shredded coconut

2 tablespoons all-purpose flour

⅛ teaspoon ground cinnamon

Dash salt

Filling

1 box (3.4 oz) instant cheesecake pudding and pie filling mix

1 cup cold 2% milk

2 cups vanilla reduced-fat ice cream, softened

1 cup chopped fresh strawberries (5 oz)

1 pint (2 cups) strawberry sorbet, softened

5 fresh strawberries, cut in half, if desired

1 Heat oven to 350°F. In medium bowl, mix all crust ingredients. Press mixture evenly in bottom and up side of ungreased 9-inch glass pie plate. Bake about 10 minutes or until golden brown. Cool completely, about 30 minutes.

2 In large bowl, beat pudding mix and milk with wire whisk until smooth. Gently stir in ice cream with wire whisk until smooth. Stir in chopped strawberries. Pour mixture into cooled crust. Freeze 2 to 3 hours or until firm.

3 Spread sorbet evenly over ice cream. Freeze 2 hours. Remove from freezer 10 minutes before serving. Cut into wedges. Garnish each wedge with strawberry half.

You'll be asked for the recipe when you serve this fantastic dessert that tastes and looks great. Gladly hand it over—what a surprise when they realize how good it is for them. Ground flaxseed, oats, walnuts and strawberries are a wonderful combination of ingredients for your health.

1 Serving: Calories 230 (Calories from Fat 70); Total Fat 8g (Saturated Fat 3.5g.); Cholesterol 15mg; Sodium 210mg; Total Carbohydrate 36g (Dietary Fiber 2g); Protein 4g

White Chocolate–Cherry Chip Ice Cream Cake

Prep Time: 25 min ▪ Start to Finish: 4 hrs 55 min ▪ 16 Servings

1 package white cake mix with
    pudding in the mix
1 box (4-serving size) white chocolate
    instant pudding and pie filling mix
1 cup water
⅓ cup vegetable oil
4 egg whites

6 cups cherry-chocolate chip ice
    cream
1 cup whipping cream
1 package (6 oz) white chocolate
    baking bars, chopped
¼ cup hot fudge topping

1 Heat oven to 350°F (325°F for dark or nonstick pan). Spray bottom only of 13×9-inch pan with baking spray with flour. In large bowl, beat cake mix, dry pudding mix, water, oil and egg whites with electric mixer on low speed 30 seconds. Beat on medium speed 2 minutes (batter will be very thick). Pour into pan.

2 Bake 28 to 30 minutes or until toothpick inserted in center comes out clean. Cool completely, about 1 hour. Meanwhile, place ice cream in refrigerator 1 hour to soften.

3 Cut cake into 1- to 1½-inch squares with serrated knife. In very large bowl, stir ice cream until very soft. Add cake squares; stir until cake is coated (cake pieces will break up). Spoon mixture back into pan. Smooth top. Freeze about 3 hours or until firm.

4 Meanwhile, in 1-quart saucepan, heat whipping cream until hot but not boiling. Stir in chopped white chocolate until melted and smooth. Pour mixture into medium bowl. Refrigerate 1½ to 2 hours or until cold.

5 Beat white chocolate mixture on high speed until soft peaks form (do not overbeat or mixture will look curdled). Spread over ice cream cake.

6 Place hot fudge topping in microwavable resealable plastic food storage bag; seal bag. Microwave on High 15 seconds or until melted; squeeze bag until topping is smooth. With scissors, cut off tiny corner of bag; gently squeeze bag to drizzle topping over cake. Serve immediately, or cover and freeze.

1 Serving: Calories 430 (Calories from Fat 200); Total Fat 22g (Saturated Fat 10g, Trans Fat 1g); Cholesterol 40mg; Sodium 400mg; Total Carbohydrate 53g (Dietary Fiber 0g); Protein 5g

Helpful Nutrition and Cooking Information

Recommended intake for a daily diet of 2,000 calories as set by the Food and Drug Administration

Total Fat	Less than 65g
Saturated Fat	Less than 20g
Cholesterol	Less than 300mg
Sodium	Less than 2,400mg
Total Carbohydrate	300g
Dietary Fiber	25g

Calculating Nutrition Information

- The first ingredient was used wherever a choice is given (such as $1/3$ cup sour cream or plain yogurt).

- The first ingredient amount was used wherever a range is given (such as 2 to 3 teaspoons).

- The first serving number was used wherever a range is given (such as 4 to 6 servings).

- "If desired" ingredients and recipe variations were not included (such as sprinkle with brown sugar, if desired).

- Only the amount of a marinade or frying oil that is absorbed by the food during preparation was calculated.

Ingredients Used in Recipe Testing and Nutrition Calculations

The following ingredients, based on most commonly purchased ingredients, are used unless indicated otherwise:

- Large eggs, 2% milk, and vegetable oil spread containing at least 65% fat when margarine is used.

- Solid vegetable shortening (not butter, margarine, or nonstick cooking spray) is used to grease pans.

Equipment Used in Recipe Testing

- Cookware and bakeware without nonstick coatings were used, unless otherwise indicated.

- No dark-colored, black or insulated bakeware was used.

- When a pan is specified, a metal pan was used; a baking dish or pie plate means ovenproof glass was used.

- An electric hand mixer was used for mixing when mixer speeds are specified.

Metric Conversion Guide

VOLUME

U.S. Units	Canadian Metric	Australian Metric
1/4 teaspoon	1 mL	1 ml
1/2 teaspoon	2 mL	2 ml
1 teaspoon	5 mL	5 ml
1 tablespoon	15 mL	20 ml
1/4 cup	50 mL	60 ml
1/3 cup	75 mL	80 ml
1/2 cup	125 mL	125 ml
2/3 cup	150 mL	170 ml
3/4 cup	175 mL	190 ml
1 cup	250 mL	250 ml
1 quart	1 liter	1 liter
1 1/2 quarts	1.5 liters	1.5 liters
2 quarts	2 liters	2 liters
2 1/2 quarts	2.5 liters	2.5 liters
3 quarts	3 liters	3 liters
4 quarts	4 liters	4 liters

WEIGHT

U.S. Units	Canadian Metric	Australian Metric
1 ounce	30 grams	30 grams
2 ounces	55 grams	60 grams
3 ounces	85 grams	90 grams
4 ounces (1/4 pound)	115 grams	125 grams
8 ounces (1/2 pound)	225 grams	225 grams
16 ounces (1 pound)	455 grams	500 grams
1 pound	455 grams	1/2 kilogram

MEASUREMENTS

Inches	Centimeters
1	2.5
2	5.0
3	7.5
4	10.0
5	12.5
6	15.0
7	17.5
8	20.5
9	23.0
10	25.5
11	28.0
12	30.5
13	33.0

TEMPERATURES

Fahrenheit	Celsius
32°	0°
212°	100°
250°	120°
275°	140°
300°	150°
325°	160°
350°	180°
375°	190°
400°	200°
425°	220°
450°	230°
475°	240°
500°	260°

NOTE: The recipes in this cookbook have not been developed or tested using metric measures. When converting recipes to metric, some variations in quality may be noted.

Index

Whatever's on the menu, make it easy with *Betty Crocker*

Betty Crocker
chicken tonight
100 Recipes for the Way You Really Cook

Betty Crocker
comfort food
100 Recipes for the Way You Really Cook

Betty Crocker
simply dessert
100 Recipes for the Way You Really Cook

Betty Crocker
outdoor food
100 Recipes for the Way You Really Cook

Betty Crocker
party food
100 Recipes for the Way You Really Cook

Betty Crocker
quick fixes
100 Recipes for the Way You Really Cook